I should have seen it coming
when the rabbit died

TERESA BLOOMINGDALE

I should have seen it coming when the rabbit died

DOUBLEDAY & COMPANY, INC.
GARDEN CITY, NEW YORK

To my parents,
Who gave me the gift of laughter.

To my husband,
Who gave me the gift of love.

To my children,
Who have enhanced both gifts a hundredfold.

God love you all.

Acknowledgments

Having one's book published is a little like receiving an Academy Award in that the author is compelled to thank all those who aided and abetted in the big event.

It is, therefore, with sincere gratitude that I give you the names of the many people who can be blamed for this book.

My heartfelt thanks to:

. . . the Religious of the Sacred Heart, who, between 1936 and 1952, forced me to create, compose, and *perfect* 962,483 essays;

. . . to the editors in my life—Robert Hoig, Robert Willems, Robert Lockwood, Robert Bonin, and, most especially, Richard B. Scheiber—whose confidence, kindness, and critiques contributed to the eventual syndication of my column;

. . . to author Arlene Rossen Cardozo, who introduced me to Doubleday;

. . . to my editor at Doubleday, Patricia Kossmann, whose patience, perseverance, and persuasion kept me from throwing my typewriter into the river;

. . . to Debbie McCann, Miss Kossmann's assistant, whose ability to see humor in everything (even this book) kept Miss Kossmann from throwing *me* into the river;

. . . and to Bart McLeay, who, when he was a cynical little seventh-grader, picked up my very first manuscript, read it . . . and laughed.

Grow old along with me!
The best is yet to be, . . .

Robert Browning

Contents

Introduction: *"The rabbit died"*

I should have seen it coming when the rabbit died.

"What do you mean: 'The rabbit died'?" I asked my obstetrician that morning in 1956. "Doesn't the rabbit always die from a pregnancy test?"

"Not this one," he replied. "I had just completed the injection when the dumb bunny jumped off the table and killed herself. Do you want to come in for another test?"

"Forget it," I sighed. "Either I'm pregnant or I've got terminal morning sickness; time will tell. There's no point in scaring another rabbit to death."

That bunny wasn't so dumb; she was just cowardly. She foresaw my future and couldn't bear to be involved. Thanks a lot, rabbit. I would think you, of all creatures, would be sympathetic to my Cause.

My Cause, that winter of 1956, was to have a big family. Married in the summer of 1955, my husband and I wanted to start our family immediately, and we planned on having a dozen children. (Lest Margaret Sanger come to haunt me, I hasten to remind you that a generation ago, it was quite acceptable, even enviable, to have a large family.)

I must be honest, however. Twenty-eight months later my Cause became clouded when our son, Michael, was born. For you see, Michael was our *third* son. Lee, III, had been born in August of 1956 (the rabbit had not died in vain); John appeared on the scene in October of 1957, and Michael came along in December of 1958. Having three sons under the age of two and a half does something to a mother, like driving her to shout:

"THERE IS NO WAY I AM GOING TO HAVE ANOTHER BABY NEXT YEAR!"

I told my husband that. I told my doctor that. I told my parents that. Fortunately, I forgot to tell God that.

In December of 1959, our fourth son, Jim, was born, followed in rapid succession by Mary (1961); Danny (1963); Peggy (1964); Ann (1966); Tim (1967); and Patrick (1969). They were not all planned, but they were all wanted, and they are all loved. This is their story, written about them and for them, and dedicated to them.

God help me if they ever read it.

Part I

Where did you come from, baby dear?
Out of the everywhere into the here.

GEORGE MACDONALD, *At the Back of the North Wind*

1

How many is too many?

Down through the years I have been asked a thousand times:

"For heaven's sake, why did you have so many children? Didn't anybody ever tell you about Planned Parenthood?"

Of course I had heard of Planned Parenthood, but in my Catholic childhood, I never knew anybody who actually *belonged* to PP. To Catholics growing up in the '30s and '40s, Planned Parenthood was like the Masonic Lodge and the PEO —selective, secretive, and verboten for Catholics. Now that I am all grown up, living in a liberated world, I know why. We were shielded from Planned Parenthood propaganda because PP failed to tell it like it is—the real and honest truth. They purport to tell how to have babies (in case anybody really wants to become a parent) and how to avoid having babies, but all they present are old-fashioned facts. They never mention the infallible, never-fail methods for modern-day mothers, or non-mothers, as the case may be.

As a service to parents, planned or unplanned, I hereby offer a brief report on the true facts concerning conception and contraception.

First, you must erase from your mind the facts of life as you learned them. They are wrong; all lies. Babies are not caused by . . . well, you know, doing *that*. If doing *that* were all it took, every couple who wanted a child would have one. No, the truth is, babies come into being when:

1. The wife finds a fascinating career which she loves and which promises prompt promotion and a brilliant future, providing she doesn't ask for a leave of absence.

2. The husband wins an all-expense-paid European Tour-for-Two, with departure date nine months from yesterday.

3. Either husband or wife forgets to pay the premium on the one insurance policy that includes maternity benefits.

4. The wife attends a Spring Fashion Show and spends her entire year's clothing allowance on four darling new outfits, all belted.

5. Husband and wife agree that three children are quite enough, so, on the birth of the third child, they sell the baby furniture and give away the maternity clothes. This is called double indemnity, for it assures the birth of at least two more children. (Who's going to buy a whole new wardrobe and a roomful of nursery furniture for just one baby?)

Those are just a few of the infallible methods for conception. If, however, you wish to avoid having babies, I suggest the following:

1. The wife must resign her well-paying job and announce to all her friends that she and her husband are going to start their family.

2. Promise your mother a grandchild for Christmas.

3. Tell your five-year-old son that he is going to have a baby brother. (This may not prevent pregnancy, but it will guarantee you a girl.)

4. Promise the school principal that, in the event that you are

not pregnant by September (though of *course* you will be), you will serve as First-Grade field-trip supervisor.

5. Spend $5,000 turning your husband's den into a nursery or, better yet, buy a bigger house.

See how easy it is? Who needs the Pill?

I never discussed the Pill with my obstetrician, for he was a devout Catholic and did not believe in any form of contraception. He believed that every baby he brought into the world was a miracle, a blessing from God, to be cherished and loved, and the more the merrier. He is an excellent doctor. He should be; I've spent a lot of years training him. I handpicked my doctor right out of medical school. He had completed his residency in Obstetrics and Gynecology the week before I was married, so I was one of his first patients. I received royal treatment every time I went to his tiny, almost-empty office. He had been a childhood friend of my husband's, so we were all on a first-name basis; very friendly, very informal, very temporary.

If there is anybody who changes color faster than a fellow's old friend who has just become a doctor, it is a doctor's old friend who is about to become a father. I later learned that there is an unavoidably strained relationship between all obstetricians and fathers-to-be based on the fact that the expectations of the doctor are exceeded only by the expectations of the father-to-be.

The father-to-be expects the doctor to be on call, twenty-four hours a day, seven days a week, for the next nine months, while the doctor expects the father to see to it that the baby arrives after breakfast and before lunch, Wednesdays and weekends being an absolute no-no.

Neither man seems to understand the indisputable facts about any pregnancy. In the first place, there has never been, in the history of motherhood, a nine-month pregnancy. Seven, sometimes; eleven, lots of times. But nine? Never. In the second place, nobody decides when the baby will be born except the baby, who will considerately give you several choices: (a) On the evening you have welcomed twelve guests to dinner and have just opened the wine and put the steaks on; (b) In the middle of the night during a raging blizzard on the day you were supposed to get the gas tank filled up and forgot; (c) During the ninth inning of the seventh game of a tied World Series.

Girl babies are more considerate than boys. When our daughter, Mary, was born in March of 1961, she announced her imminent arrival at seven-thirty on a Sunday morning. The doctor was upset, another Sunday spoiled. My husband was frantic. Who in their right mind would come to baby-sit on a Sunday with four boys ages one, two, three, and four? I, of course, was delighted, as would be any mother who has just realized that she is not going to have to cook and clean up after a Sunday dinner.

While my doctor fumed and my husband fussed and I happily packed my bag, Mary bowed to majority (male chauvinistic!) rule and went back to sleep. Thus I was allowed to spend my "day of rest" chasing and changing baby boys and picking up after same. It was not until eight-thirty that night, after her brothers had been bathed and bedded down, that Mary timidly asked permission to be born. Her father never forgot her thoughtfulness, and I never forgave it.

I must admit that both my husband and my doctor were always concerned about getting me to the hospital "on time." Of course, their concern dwindled somewhat with each delivery. When our first child was born, my nervous husband rushed me to the hospital where we were met by my doctor, anxiously awaiting my arrival. Both of them stayed by my side during a long labor, though I didn't appreciate their thoughtful concern; I slept through the entire ordeal.

By the time my sixth child was ready to be born, both husband and doctor had obviously concluded that an old pro like me needed no particular care or concern. My doctor, who by this time had a thriving practice, arrived in the delivery room thirty seconds before the baby did, patted my hand, and said cheerfully:

"Everything's going to be just fine, Dorothy."

My husband, who had driven me to the hospital and handed me over to the labor-room nurses, went on to the office, worked all day, went home, and asked the kids:

"Where's your mother?" He had forgotten.

I must admit that both men in my maternity life shaped up a bit by the time my tenth baby was born. With this delivery, my husband was the enthusiastic one ("The IRS isn't going to believe this!"), while my doctor was a nervous wreck. This was the baby I "couldn't have and shouldn't have." I was "too old, too busy, too tired." I "could die having this baby."

As you may have guessed, I didn't die. And our Patrick is the living proof that the baby you "couldn't have, shouldn't have," and maybe even determined that you wouldn't have is the prize package, the reward, the bonus blessing. I hope and pray that when my own children marry, they remember that ancient adage: "Man and woman make love, but only God can make a baby."

2

Belted is beautiful

"This is the New Look," said the salesclerk last Monday as she handed me a silk tent-shaped dinner dress. I handed it right back to her and told her to bring me something slim and slender, cinched at the waist, preferably with a belt.

"But belted is out," she exclaimed. "The full look is now the fashion."

"It would be," I sighed. "And when I had a built-in full look, the fashion was Twiggy."

I don't care what present or future fashion decrees, I shall never again don a shift, a smock, or anything at all that bears a faint resemblance to maternity modes. After ten pregnancies in twelve years, I had to call in the FBI to find my waistline, and now that I have found it, I'm not about to hide it under a blouse-on or overblouse.

I didn't always feel that way, of course. In my first pregnancy I could hardly wait to don those cute little maternity smocks. I had never before splurged on three outfits in one shopping spree, and like most women with new clothes, I wanted to wear them immediately. As I was only in my second month, I really didn't need a maternity smock, but who cared? They were so cute!

Six months later I hated the sight of the things; I had worn my one and only party shift so many times it was a disaster dress. The dress hadn't drooped; on the contrary, it was like new. Maternity clothes must be made for Catholics; the awful things (the clothes, not the Catholics) wear forever, no matter how often you wash them, stuff them in the back of the attic, or send them off to your sister. No, the disaster was in my attitude toward the dress: BLAAHHH!

My fifth pregnancy was different from my first in that I needed maternity clothes by the sixth week, but didn't get into them until the sixth month because my entire maternity wardrobe had been dispersed to my three married sisters. Sharing maternity clothes with sisters is a good idea, unless you are Catholics. If there is anything more frustrating than practicing rhythm (they call it "practicing" because you *never* perfect it), it is practicing rhythm in cadence with three sisters who are also practicing rhythm. . . . "Okay, Madeleine, you can plan a baby for March, 'cause I won't need the maternity clothes till spring, which means that Betsy can plan on Christmas and Janet will either have to wait till next year or buy her own clothes." I always felt that Janet deserved her very own maternity clothes; as the youngest of five sisters she was a permanent hand-me-down. When my mother asked Janet what she wanted for her sixteenth birthday, my baby sister had answered: "A coat without a frayed collar or Kleenex in the pockets!"

By my tenth pregnancy I didn't care what I wore, as long as I didn't have to go out and buy it. In desperation, I sent out an SOS to my sisters, who responded with boxes and boxes of clothes, unfortunately, all of them too-familiar disasters. Today they are all safely stored in the attic; I'm not about to give them away, and if you don't know why, go back and read chapter 1.

If there is anything more repugnant to an expectant mother

than the eighth-time-around maternity clothes, it is the first-, second-, or tenth-time-around maternity questions asked by well-intentioned idiots who either never were, never intend to be, or can't remember being in that condition. Following are some questions which every mother-to-be is asked at some time or other during her pregnancy, and my suggestions for answers.

(1) "Oh, my dear, so soon?" There is really no excuse for this question, unless the wedding was last Thursday and the one asking the question is your mother, in which case you can only blush, nod, and make the best of it. In any other circumstance, you should give a delighted and proud "Yes, isn't it marvelous?" unless you would prefer to punch them in the nose, in which case I would be happy to hold your coat.

(2) "Do you want a boy or a girl?" Do not, under any circumstances, answer this question. If you say you want a girl, and have a boy, somebody is bound to tell him over and over through the years: "Now I know why your mother wanted a girl." The same goes for vice versa. If you feel you must answer this question, I recommend either of two answers: (a) "Not particularly" or (b) "Of course," depending on how nauseous you have been that day.

(3) "When is the baby due?" Nobody but God knows the answer to this question, and He never tells. Some doctors will give their pregnant patients a specific due date, but these doctors are only guessing and they will be the first to admit it. It is always a good idea to tell your family and friends that the baby is due about six weeks earlier than you really expect it; this keeps them concerned and helpful during your last few weeks "of confinement." (I love that term; these days a mother in her tenth month is "confined" to the supermarket, church, the playground, kindergarten carpool, et cetera.) Unfortunately, keeping your family and friends concerned leads them to ask still another galling question:

(4) "Are you still home?" This, when you have just answered the phone and are obviously still at home. My recom-

mended answer to this question, especially if it is asked for the twelfth time by the same person: "This is a recording; at the sound of the beep, go soak your head."

(5) "Not again?" This question used to be reserved for the mother of many; today's mother can expect to hear it on her second or third pregnancy. As many times as I heard this question, you would think that I could have come up with a suitable answer, but the only comeback I ever had was: "Not again . . . still." You would be amazed at the number of people who believed me, but under the circumstances, who could blame them?

(6) "What are you going to name the baby?" Every parent has a favorite name picked out for a son or daughter, but if you are wise you will keep it a secret till the baby is born or, better yet, till baby is christened. Never name a baby you haven't met; the fact is, you may not get the baby you thought you were going to get.

This happened to us in 1958 when our third child was born. We had chosen the name James for a boy, and Mary for a girl. The morning our baby son was born, my husband came into my hospital room and said:

"I've got some disturbing news for you, honey. That baby isn't Jimmy."

"Well it certainly isn't Mary!" I said. "What do you mean: 'It isn't Jimmy'?"

"Wait till the nurse brings the baby," he replied, "and you'll see what I mean." A few moments later, the nurse brought our baby, and sure enough, he wasn't Jimmy.

"You're right," I told my husband as I cuddled our perfect baby boy. "This is a beautiful baby, but it isn't our Jim."

"Are you inferring that this isn't your baby?" the nurse asked haughtily. "This hospital does not make mistakes."

"We know that," explained my husband. "We just said this baby isn't Jimmy. Look at him! He doesn't even *look* like Jimmy!"

The nurse backed hastily out of the room, to report me, I suppose, to the staff psychiatrist.

"If this isn't Jimmy," I said to my husband, "who is he? There is no question about the fact that he is ours; just look at him!" I laughed as I held the baby up for his father's inspection. The baby, like his brothers before him, and his brothers and sisters to follow, was the spitting image of his father. (And isn't that a shame, when they have such a lovely mother?)

"Let me think about it," my husband said as he kissed me good-by. "I'll see you tomorrow."

The next morning he bounded into my hospital room, excited and somewhat relieved.

"I stopped by the nursery," he said, "and I recognized our baby immediately. He's Michael!" And of course he was Michael; still is, in fact. I don't know why we didn't recognize him immediately; he looked just like Michael. I'm certainly glad we didn't try to name him Jim; for twelve months later, Jim was born. Wouldn't it have been awful if we had given his name to someone else?

Another suggestion which I am sure no one will pay any attention to is: Never give your children rhyming names. Nobody warned us about this, and as a consequence, we have a Jim and a Tim, a Dan and an Ann. When I call "Jim!" I get an answer from Tim; if I call "Ann!" I hear from Dan, who, for some reason, never seems to be around if I call "Dan!" Or maybe he is and has decided to let Ann answer; since she insists on being a feminist, let her be the one to carry out the garbage.

Never give children names that *might* be rhymed. There are two tiny brothers in our block named Dirk and Eric. I absent-mindedly call them Derek and Eric, which isn't as bad as my teenagers, who insist on calling them Dirk and Erk. Knowing how nicknames sometimes stick, I fear that darling little Eric will be Erk forever, or at least till he's old enough to fight back.

Never give a baby a male-female name: Pat, Chris, Joe, Kelly, Bobby, Billie, Mickey, et cetera. A little girl won't mind, but a little boy will hate you forever. Our Patrick answered to Pat until the day he went to school and met three other Pats, all Patricias. Since then he has been Patrick. Patrick is a loyal little boy; he didn't blame me for his name; he just decided it was Patricia's mother who was whacky.

Oddly enough, a male-female name never seemed to bother our son Lee, probably because he had a bigger problem. He was burdened with my biggest no-no name of all: junior. I don't mean we called him Junior; I mean he was a junior, named for his father. What do you call a junior if not Junior? We called him Little Lee, which was okay until he entered kindergarten, and for some strange reason, none of the other five-year-olds called him Little Lee. Thus began years of confusion. By fourth grade, little voices were calling on the phone to threaten: "Tell Lee I'm gonna punch him in the nose!" It was fairly obvious they meant Little Lee. Three or four years later we began to get calls from big voices, saying: "Your Lee is becoming a problem; he keeps teasing the girls in the classroom." This is even more disconcerting when you realize that Big Lee was, at that time, a teacher.

The teenage years were frustrating, for by then *all* the calls were for Little Lee. At least, I assume they were, as they were all from breathless, giggling females.

But the confusion reached chaotic proportions when Little Lee became an adult-living-with-his-parents and the proud owner of his own charge accounts. The phone calls then came from credit departments, and *neither* Lee would answer the phone. It didn't really make any difference, for as every father of a young-adult-living-at-home knows: It matters not who takes the calls, it's Dad who pays the bills.

When Little Lee got married, we were still calling him Little Lee, and he respectfully requested that we change that. To what? Harry? The problem will solve itself, of course, when Little Lee has his own little Lee, for then I can call my Little Lee Middle Lee. (If I stay sober, that is.)

Of course, I could call him Arthur, for that's his other name, but we never used it because we didn't want to confuse him with his Uncle Arthur, or his grandfather whose name was Arthur; in fact, both his grandfathers were named Arthur, and his cousin is named Arthur. . . .

I wonder why I didn't think of Harry in the first place. . . .

3

But when do I sleep?

I don't know what God was thinking of when He made me a
mother. According to the rule books, I have done everything
wrong, and that's not easy, when every new rule book contra-
dicts the preceding one. It amazes me now, as I look at my ten
healthy children, that they have survived my bungling.

I wasn't always a bungler. In the beginning I did everything
"right," and the poor baby almost died of "perfection."

My first mistake was buying Dr. Spock's book on baby care.
Now I don't question Dr. Spock's methods (though I understand he himself did, in later years), it's just that I spent too
much time reading the baby book and not enough time rocking
the baby.

My second mistake was investing in all those things which are
"absolute necessities for the new baby." Standard crib, bassinette, bathinette, playpen, high chair, low chair, jump chair,
rocking chair, infant seat, car seat, baby spoon, baby dish,
sweaters, caps, booties and blankets (for a baby born in August!), undershirts, overshirts, pants and plastic pants, night-

gowns and pajamas (don't ask me why he needed both), plus a three-piece pinstripe suit, white shirt, and bow tie. The photograph of him at eight months old, in that pinstripe suit (which fit for almost a week) embarrasses him more today than a bare-bottom picture ever could.

Then there was the diaper bag, diaper pail ($5.98; it was an eighty-eight-cent bucket with a decal), baby scale, sterilizer, comb and brush, crib mobiles, and 427 toys "for infants up to twelve months," which could not be understood by anyone lacking a degree in engineering.

The only sensible buy I made was four dozen diapers, which, if they were allowed to surface in department stores today, would put Pampers and their peers out of business. It may be hard for a modern mother to believe, but 1956 cloth diapers were washable, reusable, soft, comfortable, fast-drying, and wore like iron. Ours lasted through ten babies, which was a good thing, because by the time Patrick was born I couldn't buy them anymore. By then, diapers were made of paper, the main attraction being that they were disposable. Disposable? Where? How? They may not be burned, and they certainly can't be flushed; I've got the plumber's bill to prove it. What do you do with the things? Bury them in the backyard?

I couldn't have kept house without those cloth diapers. Whatever do modern mothers use for rags? My mother suggested I use the children's underwear. I'd be happy to, if I could figure out how to get it off the children.

As I made use of my cloth diapers, so did I make use of my deluxe layette . . . though not as a layette. I couldn't put the second baby in the bassinette, as it was always full of clothes waiting to be ironed. The bathinette held folded diapers, and the playpen was stacked with toys. (Where else do you put 427 toys?) The sweaters, caps, and booties I gave as gifts to mothers of winter babies, and the "Size 6 months to a year" baby clothes (which wouldn't have fit a baby dwarf) served three terms as doll clothes. Actually, they were cheaper than doll clothes.

My dumbest purchase was the bathinette. Too big for our bathroom, it had to be set up in the bedroom, and buckets of water had to be hauled from bathroom to bedroom to fill the bathinette. After baby's bath, of course, the water had to be drained, bucketful by bucketful, and hauled back to the bathroom. The only positive aspect of the bathinette was the height; it was perfect for dressing the baby. But then, so was the kitchen counter.

Gads. I've done it now. I've admitted to dressing the baby on the kitchen counter. But it gets worse; I also bathed my babies in the kitchen sink. For shame. I didn't know this was "against the rules" until years later when I read in a newspaper column that "it is extremely unsanitary to bathe your baby in the kitchen sink." The article did not state whether it was unsanitary for the baby, or unsanitary for the sink, and now I'll never know. For while it's true that my "babies" are alive and well and as sanitary as one might expect of present-day adolescents, I can't verify the condition of the sink, for before it could succumb to babies' germs, my sink got carried away by a tornado. Don't I have all the luck?

Parents are funny people. When I was a baby, my father sang to me so I would go to sleep by seven o'clock. When I was in grade school, my mother let me "stay up" till eight-thirty. In my teenage years, both parents spent half of every evening asking:

"Good heavens, aren't you in bed yet? You've got to get more sleep!"

They sent me to college where the dorm rules demanded "Lights Out at 10:00" and God help the girl who disobeyed and studied her history notes by penlite.

Yet, oddly enough, my parents and the good nuns all claimed to be preparing me for motherhood. This is a preparation for motherhood? Teaching us to get some sleep? They should have been teaching us to stay awake.

A new mother might as well forget everything she learned about sleep. From the very moment that Number One bundle of joy joins the family, your nights are shot. The new baby wakes for feedings at two and five, and a pox on the pediatrician who will try to tell you that a baby who sleeps till 5 A.M. has "slept through the night." The night is not through at 5 A.M. Mother may be through, but the night isn't.

So after falling into bed at midnight, a new mother can expect to be up at one-thirty or two o'clock for feeding, changing, and burping (which, depending on your degree of success or failure, may necessitate more changing). With any luck at all, you can get back to bed by three-thirty, only to get up again in an hour or so for the five-o'clock feeding, after which you won't get back to bed at all because by then it's breakfast time for the Cause of it all.

In your innocence and exhaustion, you may tell yourself that things will get back to normal when Baby gets a little older, but you're wrong. Things won't get back to normal until Baby gets married. For as Baby gets older, you merely progress from the nighttime feedings to nighttime earaches, and kicking-off-the-covers, and better-check-to-see-if-he's-breathing.

By the time he is old enough to convince you that he can breathe without supervision, he will be into the terrible twos, which is always accompanied by a terrible thirst. For the next year or two you will have to get up several times each night to get him a drink of water, and since he is still a little-bitty guy and can't hold all that water (you were the one who wanted him out of diapers, Dum-Dum), you will have to get up again to take him to the potty.

Baby will outgrow this at about three or four, but by that time he will undoubtedly have a little brother or sister requesting the pleasure of your company at 2 A.M. and 5 A.M., and there you go all over again.

Eventually, of course, you will stop having babies. (Even I quit having babies,) and you will think:

"At last! I can get some sleep!"

Forget it. You have just begun to wake. For just about the

time your youngest baby begins sleeping through the night, your oldest baby begins to stay out half the night, and you will be back to walking the floor and wondering if you are *ever* going to get some sleep.

As I was thirty-nine when Patrick was born, I figure I will be sixty before I can count on getting a good night's sleep.

Maybe.

I just read an article which said that women over sixty often have difficulty sleeping. I'm not surprised. By that time they have forgotten how.

4

Cribs and crawlers and concrete Pablum

Despite the fact that they have a tendency to overflow from every orifice, babies are beautiful and are probably the best idea God ever had. Can you imagine what it would be like had God decided to create man at some other stage, say, seven years old? Two front teeth missing, bubble gum in their hair, mud under the fingernails, and a stream of questions spouting from a chocolate-covered mouth? Or at sixteen? Six feet of blue jeans, tangled hair, and acne, with goggles for eyes, headphones for ears, and two stumbling feet encased in foul-smelling, fashionably torn tennies?

Yes, God certainly knew what He was doing when He created man in the form of a cute, huggable, loving little infant, who (an added bonus!) doesn't even know how to talk! I love babies. Doesn't everybody? Who can resist a tiny creature snuggling up your shoulder, reaching for your face with his tender little hand, enjoying the very closeness of you? A baby, unlike a ten-year-old or teenager, will let you hug him and not pull away; he will submit to your kisses and coos without a smart comeback;

he will listen to your lullabies and never, ever say: "Julie Andrews you ain't." Babies are specifically sized to appeal to Mamas so that by the time your "baby" is tracking mud across your kitchen floor to hang on your refrigerator door and grumble: "Watcha got to eat?" you are so head over heels in love with him you can hardly bring yourself to say:

"Wipe your feet! You're not eating again! Have you done your homework? When are you going to get your hair cut?"

However, I must be a realist; babies are not always sweet, as I was reminded by our son Lee, when he and Karen were planning their wedding.

"You've got to be kidding!" I heard him shout at her, as they pored over plans at the kitchen table.

"Why should I be kidding?" she asked, puzzled. "It makes a beautiful bridal bouquet, and it's not expensive, if that's what you are worried about!"

"What's the matter?" I asked, despite my determination not to be an interfering mother-in-law-to-be.

"Listen to this, Ma," said my son. "Karen wants to carry a bridal bouquet made up of baby's breath! I've never seen it, but I can sure imagine what it smells like!"

I assured my son, who as the eldest of ten children is as wise about babies as he is ignorant about flowers, that "baby's breath" is a misnomer.

"I should hope so!" he sighed in relief, as he recalled the many times he had bottle-fed (and burped) a baby brother or sister.

A friend of ours, who is the father of nine grown children, once remarked how he missed "the sweet smell of the crib." I think he was a little kooky, but maybe you get like that when the kids are finally gone and you find yourself living in a din of silence. My memories of the nursery are not all that nostalgic.

While legend would have it that babies spend their waking hours lying peacefully in their cribs, dreamily watching mobiles, or tenderly hugging teddy bears, the fact is, most babies devote their conscious hours to contemplating ways to destroy their cribs. The strength and ingenuity of a ten-pound, twenty-inch baby boy is incredible. Simply by lying on his tummy and shifting his weight, he can, in a matter of minutes, move his crib across the room till it hits the wall. Total destruction, however, may not come until several months later, when he learns to kneel up in his crib. By then he can not only steer it to the wall, he can, by swaying back and forth, bang the crib repeatedly until either the crib or the wall collapses.

If the crib withstands the constant banging, it will nevertheless succumb to perpetual scrubbing. I cannot believe that I am the only constant crib-scrubber in the world, but I may be, due to the fact that I never perfected the art of "securing the diaper." Because I never pinned a diaper properly, our babies found it very simple to step out of their diapers . . . which they always did at the most inopportune moments. The resulting disaster never bothered Baby, who often took advantage of the occasion to indulge in a little poopy pie-making, thereby bringing cries from older brothers and sisters (my reluctant clean-up crew) of: "Oh, no, not another poopy party!"

While the older kids became experts on cleaning the crib, they never learned how to clean the high chair. For that matter, neither did I. I don't know what ingredients are incorporated into baby cereal, but I recommend the formula to concrete companies, or whoever is in charge of building our streets and highways. A spoonful of baby cereal, when slobbered upon the chrome arm of a high chair, will, in a matter of minutes, harden into a cementlike substance guaranteed to last a lifetime.

Although I endured ten infancies, I never acquired the art of successfully spoon-feeding a baby. Spoon-feeding tiny babies did not become fashionable until the mid-1950s, just in time for my firstborn. Prior to that time, babies were bottle- or breast-fed until they were old enough to make their own peanut butter and jelly sandwiches. But around 1956, some pediatrician, who was obviously not a parent, decided that every four-week-old baby should eat carrots, spinach, green beans, and a variety of other vegetables and fruits, all of which were cooked and strained to the consistency, attractiveness, and taste of soggy sand.

How does one go about spoon-feeding a four-week-old baby? Obviously, the baby cannot sit in a high chair. You *can* place him in an infant seat, which is perfect for him, unless your baby happens to have feet, in which case he will scoot himself and seat right off the edge of the table. I found I had no recourse but to hold the baby on my lap, anchoring him with one hand, while with my other hand I would dip the spoon into the dish and thus into Baby's mouth. In another hand I would hold a towel to wipe up the gallon of spat goo which Baby could somehow produce from a teaspoonful of strained spinach, and with my other hand I would hold a bottle of milk, ready to pop into Baby's mouth, thereby forcing him to swallow the spinach.

If you have assumed from the above that I have more than the prescribed number of hands, you are correct. Every mother is given an extra pair of hands with the birth of her first child. These extra hands are exceedingly useful, through the years, for grabbing toddlers when the car brakes suddenly, hugging several sensitive siblings all at the same time, and holding a telephone while simultaneously signaling to a teenager that if he takes those car keys off that shelf you will break his arm. Mother's extra arms are not visible, but believe me, they are there. Ask any mother.

Some grandparents would have us believe that the sweetest sound in the world is a baby's coo. They are wrong. The sweetest sound is a baby's burp, especially if it is three in the morning and Momma or Daddy is dying to get back to bed. All newborn babies awake in the middle of the night for a feeding. I know you have heard some parents claim that "our Billy slept through the night from the very beginning." If you know such a parent, cut him off quickly and avoid him like the plague. He is the type who will tell you, through the years, that Billy was potty-trained at three months, walked six weeks later, and spoke two languages by his first birthday. It will get worse as Billy excels his way through kindergarten, cub scouts, an acne-free adolescence, and Harvard Graduate School, to which he earned a full scholarship just for being Billy.

This is not to say you should avoid Billy, who will probably grow up to be an affable, carefree person with delightfully delinquent kids. But steer clear of his parents . . . forever. If you think they are bad now, wait till they get to be grandparents.

There is a special place in heaven for a parent who, on hearing the newborn cry at night, says to her or his spouse: "Don't get up, honey. I'll feed him." Since we had our babies in the days before Betty Friedan taught husbands how to hold a baby bottle, I was the saint who got up at night and stumbled downstairs to a cold, dark kitchen to warm the bottle (don't doze or it will overheat), test the temperature (it did; run it under cold water; it'll break and you get to start all over), and climb back up to the nursery to feed the baby. Feeding the baby, of course, is only a small part of it. First you must change Baby, then feed him, then change him all over because he spits up, then feed him some more because you want to be sure he got enough to eat, then walk the floor to get him to go back to sleep while you keep patting his back and praying: "Please, God, let him burp so I can go back to bed." Did my babies cooperate? Never. I paced; I patted; I rubbed. Baby would just snuggle into my shoulder and snore. I'd shake; I'd shout; I'd toss him into the air. He slept on. Finally I would give up, place him gently in his crib, tiptoe back to bed, settle myself gratefully between the sheets, and "WAAA!!!" Baby would wail. And why not? He was full of gas.

Parents are contrary creatures. We spend the first year of Baby's life waiting for him to talk, and the next twenty years wishing he would shut up. Why are we so anxious to hear that first word? For the simple reason that every mother hopes the first word will be "Mama," and every father prays it will be "Daddy." Give up, Mother. The first word is *always* "Daddy."

The fact is, the first sound any baby makes is "Da." Baby is so delighted to hear the sound of his own voice, he repeats himself: "Da-da-da-da." You may wonder, as many mothers have wondered before you, how the nickname "daddy" ever came from "father." Now you know. Some enterprising prehistoric papa confiscated prehistoric baby's first word: Da-da.

In my opinion, every pair of parents should be allowed one kid to practice on. This could be arranged by God's allowing unrepentant sinners who have died and gone to purgatory to serve out their punishment by being reincarnated as firstborn children. We parents make so many mistakes with our firstborn children, burdening them with so many "blessings," it is amazing that they survive our tender loving care.

Our first baby was born in the month of August. Ten days later, though it was 102 degrees in the shade, I swaddled him in undershirt, diapers, plastic pants, knit kimono, sweater, cap, booties, and blanket just to drive him three blocks to church for his baptism. He was the only baby I ever saw who smiled in appreciation when the cool, christening waters were poured over his steaming brow.

Throughout his infancy, our firstborn was fed the "perfect" formula, carefully measured into thoroughly sterilized bottles. We sterilized everything; I spent half of each day dipping rubber duckies, blocks, and baby rattles into hot water because they had touched the floor, and might touch Baby's mouth. Baby had his own dishes, his own toilet articles, his own toilet . . . a cute little potty chair with padded back, painted decals, and built-in toys. His wardrobe was so handsome, so complete, so expensive, it might have been custom-ordered from Bloomingdale's in New York.

In spite of it all, he survived such "blessings" and grew into a perfectly normal, repulsive adolescent.

His siblings were not so burdened. By the time we had spoiled five babies, and were down to Number Six, our Dan had a wardrobe which obviously came from Bloomingdale's of

Omaha: two undershirts (size six washed down to a size two), two pair of crawlers with built-in knee holes, and no shoes. Why buy shoes for a kid who can't walk? I stopped forcing my babies into high-topped, high-priced, hard-soled shoes the day I saw a "first birthday portrait" of Nelson Rockefeller's baby . . . barefoot. What's good enough for Happy is good enough for me; from then on, our babies went barefoot till kindergarten time.

Danny shared his dish with the puppy, his toys with all his brothers and sisters, and he didn't have to share his potty for the simple reason that he didn't have one. I had long since given up on potty-training an infant. By child Number Three or Four, I had discovered that if I diligently watched the clock and took Baby to the potty at regular intervals, spending hours sitting on the edge of the tub, prodding and praying and persuading and praising, I could train the baby by the time he was eighteen months old. On the other hand, if I ignored the whole thing, Baby would, by observation, train himself by the time he was two. So what's six months? I had spent that long sitting on the edge of the tub. So the second half of our family never got toilet-trained, yet as far as I know, they are all out of diapers.

After my first baby, I stopped sterilizing everything, including the formula. I discovered that mother's milk is not only healthier, it is also easier to heat and serve. Toys which had been kicked under the sofa and retrieved by the dog were cheerfully chewed on by toddlers who thrived under conditions which would have horrified the health department. It only took about three toddlers for me to realize that a baby who crawls all over the floor and then sucks his thumb, without dying from dysentery, will not be contaminated by sharing an ice-cream cone with the dog. Of course, I can't guarantee the continuing health of the dog, but that's not my problem. Any dog that's dumb enough to follow a dirty-fingered, jelly-smeared, damp-panted baby around, demanding his turn at the teething ring, deserves what he gets.

Despite the dirty fingers, the baby stage is the most delightful age of all. The joy of teaching a baby to walk and talk is an indescribable one, enhanced only when there are older children to share that joy with. If there is anything more inspiring than watching a new baby sleeping in his crib, it is watching an "old baby" watching the new baby sleeping in his crib. A two-year-old standing on tiptoe, peeking into the crib; a four-year-old on hands and knees, laughingly trying to teach the baby to crawl; a six-year-old sitting beside the baby's bed, thoughtfully considering the intricacies of a tiny baby's ear; an eight-year-old trying to teach his baby brother how to hold a football; a ten-year-old tenderly placing her favorite doll in baby sister's bassinette; a twelve-year-old awkwardly and surreptitiously lifting his baby sister from her crib for a quick but loving hug . . . these are the things that make motherhood wonderful and will, I hope, explain once and for all, Why I had so many kids.

Part II

If you can keep your head when all about you
Are losing theirs and blaming it on you;
If you can trust yourself when all men doubt you
But make allowance for your doubting too . . .

Then you're a mama!

RUDYARD KIPLING, "If"

5

The broken home

If mothers perfect any talent during their tenure as mothers, it is the ability to worry well. With ten children, I have become a professional worrier, a fact which panics my husband since he read someplace that "worriers tend to die younger than non-worriers." This, of course, is nonsense. If that were true, there wouldn't be any living grandmothers. None of them would have survived as mothers.

A mother cannot expect to start right out as a professional worrier; you must first fulfill an apprenticeship, which begins the moment your obstetrician says: "Congratulations, my dear, you are going to become a mother." For the next nine months, you will worry that your baby might not be hale and hearty, that he might be born with his father's looks and your brains (or vice versa), that he might dare to be born during the Super Bowl game.

Once Baby arrives, healthy and handsome, bright and beautiful, and right on schedule (during the fourth quarter) you cannot stop worrying. You must move on to other worries: Is he breathing? Is he growing? Why does he eat so much? Why won't he eat more? Why does he crawl crooked?

As a matter of fact, one of our babies did crawl crooked; Annie crawled sideways. We had her tested for everything from brain damage to knock-knees before her grandmother finally found the cause of the crooked crawling. My mother had been baby-sitting all afternoon for me, and when I came home, as Grandma kissed seven or eight kids good-by, patted the poodle, and shoved the Irish setter aside, she turned to me and said: "No wonder Annie crawls sideways; something or somebody is always in her way."

You will finally worry your crawler onto his feet only to find that now you have to worry about how high he can reach, how fast he can run, and oh-my-God, what did he flush down the toilet this time?

By the time your toddler is three, he will be demanding independence, which means he will want to play outside without being tied to the porch post. So you will spend the next two years worrying that he will go out into the street, ride his trike through the neighbor's tulips, or get clobbered by the naughty little boy next door. On alternate days, you will worry because he *is* the naughty little boy next door, picking on the neighbor's now-reformed children.

With great relief you will send him off to school, only to spend the primary grades worrying because he makes funny 5s, adds when he should subtract, and can never remember how to spell his last name.

During the middle grades your worries are pretty much confined to whether or not he is going to outgrow his winter coat before spring, assuming, of course, that he can *find* his winter coat. (Have you looked behind the refrigerator? In the doghouse? On the car floor? Maybe even . . . in his closet?)

Then comes junior high, and you will worry, along with him, that he is growing up to be too short or too tall, too fat or too thin, or will he ever grow up at all?

Only when he enters high school can you attain your status of professional worrier. Are they really going to let that fumble-fingered fourteen-year-old take chemistry? Surely he will blow up the school! (The thought will occur to him.) Go out for football? Stay out till midnight? Where is he? With whom?

At sixteen, he will start to drive, and now, along with worrying about *him,* you also get to worry about your car, the people in it, all the other cars in the area, and the steadily rising premiums on your auto insurance.

Finally, he will grow up and go to college. Now you no longer have to worry that he won't brush his teeth or say his prayers; instead you will worry that he will study too hard, or worse, not hard enough; that he will get married too soon, or worse, not soon enough; that he will want to move out and get his own apartment; or worse, that he will never move out at all.

Nobody worries more than a mother, yet mothers live longer than anybody. Why? Because as her children grow up and mother grows older, she switches from worrying to praying, and then she becomes indispensable, and God lets her live longer. For God well knows that if there is anyone more precious to a family than a mother who worries, it's a grandmother who prays.

The most worrisome age has to be the toddler stage. I know that mothers of older children tend to tell mothers of toddlers: "If you think it's hard now, wait till they get to be teenagers!" thus throwing mothers of toddlers into a state of panic and depression. But the truth is, the toddler stage is the hardest of all; mothers of teenagers have just mercifully forgotten it. I had both toddlers and teenagers at the same time, and I'll opt for the teen years. When a teenager gets into trouble, or goofs off, mother can say: "It's your own fault; you know better." But if the toddler paints the dining room wall or knocks over the refrigerator, guess who his daddy blames?

If God holds me responsible for the antics of my toddlers, I will spend eternity in purgatory. I shudder to recall the toddler years. . . .

. . . The time Michael, then two years old, stuffed Kleenex into the upstairs bathroom sink, turned on the water, and departed. I was sitting on the front-porch steps enjoying the beautiful spring day, negligently unaware of my toddler's activities until three-year-old John came out and asked:

"Mommy, why is it raining in the dining room?" The chandelier, dripping water from every prism, was a spectacular sight. So was the ceiling when it fell.

. . . The Easter Sunday my husband said: "I'm bored; think I'll go for a walk." He followed the fire trucks home. Our four-year-old Lee had found a book of matches and, after four or five unsuccessful strikes, finally managed to ignite the front porch. Did my little arsonist run away, to hide in the bushes and cry in shame? He did not. He walked straight over to his mother, put his little hand in mine, and courageously admitted:

"John did it."

Poor John spent most of his preteen years taking the blame for Lee's antics, until one summer twelve-year-old John suddenly realized that by some miracle he had outgrown his thirteen-year-old brother, so, without word or reason, he simply beat the hell out of him. Did things change? Yes. From then on they both blamed Michael.

. . . The time four-year-old Lee, while watching television, decided to help the good guys catch the bad guys. He grabbed his water pistol, shot at the bad guys through the back of the TV set, and blew up the picture tube, all the transistors, and my nervous system.

. . . The morning our three-year-old Patrick and his buddy Jacob climbed into the front seat of my car, released the brake, and rolled off down the street toward a federal highway. It took two frantic guardian angels to steer the car into a neighbor's bushes and return the two unconcerned little demons to their panic-stricken mothers.

. . . The day Patrick, then about four, slammed the door on his finger, reached down to pick up whatever-it-was that fell, and realized it was his finger. He coolly picked it up and brought it to me, saying: "Fix it, Mommy." A kind friend drove to the hospital; a good doctor fixed the finger; a frantic Mommy fainted.

. . . The day Mike, John, and Lee, then about five, six, and seven years old, found a footlocker full of old letters in Mr. Neighbor's garage and, along with Mr. Neighbor's six-year-old, played mailman, happily distributing them to every mailbox in the block. Unfortunately, the letters were old love letters Mr. Neighbor had received some twenty years before, in his single days in the Navy. To make matters worse, the letters were not from the girl who became Mrs. Neighbor. I learned a lesson from that embarrassing experience. I burned my old love letters.

The toddler years are terrible, because toddlers, cute as they are, must be watched every minute of every day or they may dismantle the entire neighborhood. Your parents will try to tell you: "Blink your eyes and they'll be all grown up," but don't you believe it. And for God's sake, don't try it. I blinked my eyes and my toddlers broke the dining-room table. It isn't easy to break a dining-room table, but they managed, and naturally, it was my fault. I had made the mistake of taking two of them with me when I shopped for the dining-room furniture, and they overheard me ask the salesman:

"Is this table sturdy? We have a lot of children, and they tend to be hard on furniture."

The salesman had replied: "Madame, six people could dance on this table and it wouldn't even wobble."

He was right. When seven-year-old John persuaded his four younger brothers and sister to join him in testing the table, it didn't wobble a bit as it was splitting right down the middle.

My toddlers broke everything they touched, usually on purpose. Given a new toy, they would take it apart to see how it worked. Or they would bounce it, or throw it, unless it was a ball meant to be bounced and thrown; *that* they would flush down the toilet.

There were times when I thought I was raising a bunch of terrorists, until one day when I was enrolling one of them in kindergarten. I was filling out the registration form and came to a question: "Describe the condition of your home. Check one: Excellent, Good, Moderate, Fair, Poor, Broken." I turned to my friend Madeleine, who was filling out the same form for her little son, and said: "Isn't this a ridiculous question? How do you answer something like that? I suppose everybody checks Moderate."

"Not I," said Madeleine. "I always check Broken."

"But why?" I asked, knowing Madeleine to be the happily married mother of seven children.

"Because everything is," she sighed. "The washing machine is broken; the TV is broken; the bikes are broken; the back door is broken. . . ."

I loved Madeleine for that remark. It has kept me sane for years.

6

You ate WHAT?

"They are so cute!" said the nurse, as she boosted the four little boys onto the table in the Emergency Ward of Children's Hospital.

"Just precious!" agreed her assistant, handing each of my four sons a basin and carefully tying bibs around their little necks.

"Okay, fellas," said the nurse cheerfully, "if you each take a little sip of this syrup, I'll give everybody a big glass of pop. Won't that be nice?"

Yeah, nice. I knew what the syrup was: Ipecac. And I just hoped the boys could hang onto the basins when the Ipecac began to bring up their breakfasts.

The "cute, precious" little boys were my terrible toddlers: Lee, four years old; John, three; Michael, two; and Jim, one. I had rushed them to Children's Hospital Poison Control Center when I found the aspirin bottle empty, and little Lee conspicuously absent. In answer to my frantic inquiries, John had related the following incident:

"Lee wanted to play hospital and he said he would be doctor

and he gave us lotsa pills and then he looked kinda scared and ran off."

I had found a trembling "physician" hiding behind the basement door and concluded that an intensive interrogation should take priority over a paddling. It was true; they had eaten aspirin, but couldn't remember how many, so it was off to Poison Control.

As the "doctor and his patients" obediently upchucked into their basins, I turned to see a familiar face in the doorway. It belonged to Lee Terry, News anchorman for one of Omaha's top television stations. To my horror, Lee was preparing his camera in order to film the upchucking.

"What are you doing here?" I cried, knowing very well what he was doing here.

"I was down the hall, covering an accident, and when I heard the nurses talking about these cute kids, I decided this will make a great human-interest story."

"Not nearly as great as the story which will follow it," I told him.

"What story is that?" he asked.

"MOTHER CLOBBERS ANCHORMAN WITH CAMERA!" I replied emphatically. "C'mon, Lee," I pleaded, "if there is anything I don't need today, it is my husband's reaction to seeing his sons throwing up all over the six o'clock news. He'd kill me."

"Yeah!" said Lee, with a twinkle in his eye, "and what a news story *that* would make!" He was teasing, and I watched with relief as he reluctantly put away his camera and even helped me lift the boys off the table and steer them out to the car.

Never underestimate the ingenuity of toddlers, as I did one summer when I took the boys to St. Joseph, Missouri, to visit my parents. My mother was well aware of her grandsons' reputation, so she had anticipated their arrival with spectacular precautions. After we had unpacked our suitcases and were preparing the boys for their naps, Mother explained to me why I need not worry about making any quick trips to the hospital.

"I gathered together everything in this house that is dangerous or poisonous," she said proudly, "and put it on the top shelf of my bedroom closet."

"That's not good enough, Mother," I told her. "They can shove a chair in that closet and scoot up those shelves as quick as monkeys."

"No, they can't," she said. "I have removed from the house every shoveable chair, ladder, stool, table, or box which might be used to boost them up to that first shelf."

"Marvelous!" I laughed, as she explained that everything had been stored in the neighbor's basement. We kissed the boys "good nap" and went downstairs to have a cup of tea.

Thirty minutes later I concluded that their naptime was just too quiet for comfort, so I went up to check on them. As I expected, they were not sleeping; most naptimes were spent wrestling with pillows or each other, laughing, shouting, but at least corralled in their bedroom. As all mothers know, naptimes are not for the benefit of the toddler; I never yet knew a toddler who needed a nap. It's *mother* who benefits from her toddler's nap. So I was not surprised to find my toddlers awake, but I was surprised to find them participating in their favorite pastime: a poison party. All four of them were seated on the floor, happily passing around pills of every color and shape. There were vitamin pills, cold tablets, aspirin, Ex-Lax, all those "goodies" that Grandma had so carefully stored on her top shelf. As we had no way of knowing how many, if any, of the poisons they had ingested, we had to take all four boys to the clinic for a repeat performance of the Ipecac experience.

"How did they get up there?" wailed my mother as we drove them downtown to the clinic. "There was nothing for them to climb on!" But of course there was, though it was understandable why she had not considered it when taking her precautions. There was our luggage; those four sturdy suitcases we had brought with us to Grandma's house. The boys had shoved each piece into the closet, carefully stacked one on top of the other, and scrambled right up to the top shelf.

Thanks to Ipecac, the kids recovered by evening; my nerves had settled down by the next morning, and the psychiatrist said Grandma would be back to normal by Christmas.

7

Is it around the next corner?

"Vacation," says Noah Webster, "is a time of respite from something; a scheduled period during which activity is suspended; a period of exemption from work granted for rest and relaxation."

Evidently Noah did not have kids. My husband and I have taken various vacations through the years, some with toddlers, some with teenagers, and some with middle kids, and the only thing that was suspended was the "rest and relaxation." The only way to relax on a vacation with kids is to take them all to Grandma's, dump them in her kitchen, and say:

"We're going up to Grandma's third floor; we'll be down on Sunday."

I have been asked often: "What is the 'best age' to take children on a trip? Are they easier as toddlers? When they are in grade school? Or do teenagers make the best travelers?"

There are two "best ages": one when the oldest child is six weeks old and will spend the entire trip sleeping in a basket on the back seat, and the other when the youngest child is thirty-three, married, with a family of her own, and would be thrilled at the prospect of an August weekend in Death Valley if it meant getting away from her own kids.

Any age in between is a bust.

When we took our toddlers on a trip, we spent half the time in roadside rest rooms, and the rest of the time trying not to hear backseat questions and comments:

"Are we almost there?" . . . "Is it over the next hill?" . . . "Why can't I sit in the front seat?" . . . "Mama, will you tell Patrick not to throw his shoes out the window?" . . . "Daddy, will you make Annie quit throwing my sweater on the floor?" . . . "Stop throwing your weight around, Dan!" . . . "Daddy, I think you'd better stop the car a minute!" . . .

"Why? Is somebody throwing something again?"

"Yes."

"Who?"

"Tim."

"What's he throwing?"

"Up!"

We took the teenagers on a vacation, spent half the time in roadside restaurants and the other half ignoring the backseat questions and comments:

"I don't see why I had to come on this dumb trip." . . . "You mean you woke me up just to look at the Grand Canyon?" . . . "When are we gonna eat?" . . . "Move over jerk; you're taking the whole back seat." . . . "Where am I supposed to put my legs? We aren't all midgets, Shorty." . . . "Hey, Dad, whyncha let me take the wheel awhile? I'll show you how to burn rubber, man!"

Families with ten children take few, if any, vacations unless they are very rich or very crazy or both. (We don't fall into the first category, and contrary to what my friends and relatives claim, we do not qualify for the second category either. At least, not often.) We have some close friends who did take their ten children on an auto trip to California. (They aren't rich, but they are a little crazy.) They took two cars, with the dad driving one, and the mother driving the other, and everything went smoothly except for one minor mishap. They inadvertently left their ten-year-old son in a rest room someplace in Nevada.

It seems that after the rest stop, they reloaded the cars, and Mom thought the boy was with Dad, while Dad thought he was with Mom. They got almost all the way to L.A. before somebody said: "Where's Joey?" After a frantic discussion, they concluded that Joey must still be in Las Vegas (probably making a bundle off a slot machine) and Mom made Dad drive back to pick him up, despite a majority vote from the rest of the family that they continue their journey and retrieve Joey on the return trip.

While our vacations *en famille* are few and far between, our kids are treated, each and every summer, to a week at Grandma's, 150 miles away, as the bus flies.

When the kids were little, my husband was working at two jobs and couldn't get away for a vacation (some excuse!), so I, fearful of highway driving, took them to Grandma's on the bus.

I don't know why there are so many cars on our Nebraska and Kansas highways because it is obvious to anyone who ever walked into a bus depot that everyone in the Midlands travels by bus. Those not traveling are meeting someone who is traveling. I have never seen an uncrowded bus station. Don't get there early, for every seat is sure to be occupied and you will have to stand. You will have to stand anyway, for the ticket lines are long, and the question is not "Must I stand?" but rather "Which line should I stand in?" It matters not which line you choose, the others will move faster.

Don't waste your time pushing the kids to the front of the departure gate in the hopes that you will be first on the bus and get the window seats; those seats are already taken. How could those people get to the window seats when the bus's journey originates here, and we are first in line? It's easy. Window-seat occupants come with the bus; they are factory-installed.

So the kids are spread out all over the bus, and I am left sit-

ting next to a fat man who snores his way to St. Joe, but that
doesn't bother me; he's not *my* fat man. I ignore those passen-
gers who *are* mine, as they run up and down the aisles, trading
seats and sandwiches, books and blows.

The bus is met by my sister, the children's Aunt Do, so-called
because, after deliberately choosing a life of Single Bliss, she has
spent most of her time "doing" things for her twenty-seven
nieces and nephews. By the end of the vacation, the kids will be
calling their Aunt Do "Aunt Don't," for during the last couple of
days she has said: "Children, please don't play football with
Grandma's crystal vase." . . . "Don't play leap-frog in the
flower bed." . . . "Don't fiddle with the color TV." . . .
"Don't wake your mother." And where is mother? On
Grandma's third floor, of course. See you Sunday!

On rare occasions, my husband and I have taken a vacation
without the children, but we discovered it's not a good idea. It's
that same old "age" problem. We can't bear to leave them when
they are little; and we don't dare leave them when they are big.

The first time we attempted a vacation without the kids was
on the occasion of our fifth wedding anniversary. My sister-in-
law had agreed to stay with our terrible toddlers while my husband and I drove to the Rocky Mountains. Some vacation. We
refer to it as our "five, fun-filled minutes in Colorado Springs."
As we registered in the hotel, my husband was handed a message: "Call home immediately." Do you know what that idiot
did? He called home! It seems all four boys had come down with
the measles, and my husband insisted we go home. That shows
how stupid you are at thirty; if we had been ten years older and
were on vacation and a sitter called to say the kids had the measles, I would have answered the phone with: "I'm sorry, but you
have reached a non-working number!"

Ten years later we took our second vacation without the kids,
and thanks to Vatican II, this one was a grand success.

When my husband had first told me that he must attend a
convention in San Francisco at which wives were included, I

told him to forget it. How could I possibly find a baby-sitter for ten kids, all under the age of fifteen? And then I had a marvelous thought! Vatican II!

Vatican II was the historical council called by Pope John XXIII to modernize the customs of the Catholic Church. One of the most traditional customs to be discarded was "the cloister." Nuns who heretofore had lived secluded lives within quiet convent walls were now leaving the cloister to go out into the world and perform charitable works. Where better than at our house?

So I called the Notre Dame Convent and arranged for two nuns to come care for the children in our absence. The kids were horrified.

"Nuns!" wailed my products of parochial schools. "You're not going to leave us, day and night, with NUNS!?"

Even I was a little dubious. How would nuns, in their long, heavy habits, manipulate their way across our cluttered rooms, or find privacy in our crowded house? Could they stand the noise? The chaos? The confusion? Would they be horrified by the habits, haircuts, and locker-room language of my sons?

A miracle occurred. The week before the nuns were to arrive, another directive of Vatican II allowed the nuns to modify their habits and even to wear casual clothes for around-the-house and recreation. Consequently, when "the sweet old dears" I was expecting arrived on the scene, we had quite a surprise. The nuns, clad in culottes, T-shirts, and tennies, were twenty-year-old novices; both came from big families with lots of brothers (they'd understand the language!) and sisters; and after two years in their all-adult novitiate, they were happily anticipating two weeks of playing with kids, raiding a refrigerator, planning picnics and games, and proving to themselves that they could be just as efficient in a kitchen as they were in a convent.

However, despite their qualifications, and their enthusiastic optimism, I had a few doubts about leaving my children with strangers, even though they were nuns, and I very quietly cautioned our eldest son, fourteen-year-old Lee, to call us in case of an emergency. He told me to forget my worries, enjoy my vacation, and be assured he would contact me if something serious arose.

Six hours later, after my husband and I had checked into the beautiful Mark Hopkins Hotel overlooking San Francisco Bay, I was changing into a gown in anticipation of cocktails at the Top of the Mark when the telephone rang. It was eldest son.

"Mother," he whispered, "you told me to call you if something serious came up."

"Yes, yes, what is it, honey?" I asked, frantic. "Speak up! I can't hear you! What's the matter?"

"Well," he hesitated, "you did tell me to call you in case of an emergency. . . ."

"Yes, I know. I did. What is it?" An auto accident? Kidnaping? The nuns were gangsters in disguise and they're holding my babies for ransom? (Of course not; if they were in disguise, they would have been wearing long black habits.) "For heaven's sakes, tell me what's happened!"

"Well," he repeated, and then blurted it out: "Sister Margaret won't let me go to the movies!"

It cost us $7.40 for the phone call, because of course we had to talk to all the kids; after all, we'd been away for six hours. And that didn't include the $30 for an elegant meal, which my husband insisted on buying me, at San Francisco's famous restaurant, Paoli's, to calm my jangled nerves. I *was* worried; not that the kids might not like the nuns, but that the nuns might not be able to manage the kids. I learned one thing in that two weeks; a nun by any other name or in any other habit is still a nun. We returned to find our kitchen chalkboard covered with a hundred messages, all reading: "I must not call my mother when she's on vacation."

It had been a marvelous vacation; we loved San Francisco . . . the shows, the shops, the art galleries. But the night life was awful. I don't mean San Francisco's night life was awful; I mean *our* night life was awful. Since neither my husband nor I are nightclubbers, our idea of a really terrific evening is to crawl into bed with a good book. Which we both did, every evening. But after one or two chapters, he would get up and pace the floor, look at the window, check the phone, then go back to his book, only to get up again after a few minutes and go through the same routine.

"What's the matter with you?" I grumbled. "Can't you settle down? I want to read my book."

"I do too," he said. "But I can't."

"Why not?" I asked.

"No interruptions!" he said. "I can't read without interruptions; I need some kids to pop in with arithmetic questions or to ask me some dumb riddle. I want to help somebody unbutton their buttons or untie their knots. I need some little faces to kiss good night! Whose idea was this dumb vacation, anyway?"

To this day he has never forgiven those kids for not coming down with the measles.

I wonder if baby-sitters realize how much we mothers appreciate them? Through the years I have been blessed with the assistance of many wonderful women and teenage girls who subjected themselves to our "sweet smelling" nursery, our terrible toddlers, our raucous grade-schoolers, our sharp-tongued teenagers. There was Mrs. Fricke, who came every Thursday for years so that I could "get out" to grocery shop, or attend a meeting, or just go for a walk by myself. Marguerite, Jewel, and Amanda, each in turn, kept order in my house and sunshine in my life. And Marcene was a darling high-school girl, who came to sit for the first time when she was thirteen and earned her halo in the next five years, returning again and again to the "battle front."

Mrs. Clemens was a grandmotherly type who came each year to stay with the children while I went to the hospital to have a baby; and of course, my own mother came, also each year, to welcome the new baby home from the hospital and to take on that first two weeks of "middle-of-the-night-feeding."

Mrs. Gilpin was another wonderful grandmotherly type, who came every Fourth of July so that my husband and I could retreat behind the lines for R and R. To celebrate our July 2 wedding anniversary, my husband and I would treat ourselves to a weekend in a local motel (close enough for emergencies; far enough for peace and quiet). Mrs. Gilpin was a lovely widow lady of undetermined years; a wonderful person, but the most trusting soul God ever created. Unfortunately, the kids realized this and spent most of that weekend pulling practical jokes.

The first time Mrs. Gilpin came to our house, we had five children: four boys and one baby girl. Instead of our usual weekend of R and R, my husband and I planned to take our princess to see my folks. On leaving written instructions for Mrs. Gilpin, I had unthinkingly made frequent references to our "five children." She naturally assumed, therefore, that she was to stay with five children.

As a consequence, when our little neighbor Bobby, playing at our house when Mrs. Gilpin arrived, wanted to go home at dinnertime, she refused to let him go.

"But I don't live here!" cried little Bobby.

"Don't give me that!" answered Mrs. Gilpin. "I've heard what jokers you boys are. You get upstairs and wash up for dinner." It wasn't until Bobby's mother came searching for him that Mrs. Gilpin reluctantly let him go.

For the next three or four years, Mrs. Gilpin was busy with her own family, so her sister Helen came instead. Unfortunately, Helen was more trusting than Mrs. Gilpin, so when my sons sneaked an extra kid in on her, Helen just assumed that little Billy was a Bloomingdale. (No mother in her right mind would name a boy Billy Bloomingdale, but Helen had already decided that I was missing a few marbles.) Billy spent most of his time at our house anyway, so his mother was not surprised when he didn't come home each evening till bedtime. Billy would pretend to go to bed with our boys, then sneak out the basement-bedroom window, dash home, and return to our house early the next morning via the same route. Helen never did catch on and, to this day, asks me about "your son, Bill; such a nice lad. Went to bed early every night and not a peep out of him till morning."

When Mrs. Gilpin returned three or four summers later, our kids had grown so much she hardly knew them. To add to the confusion, our family had increased by three or four. I can't remember exactly whether it was three or four, and evidently Mrs. Gilpin couldn't either, for when suppertime rolled around, she told our son John to go home.

"But Mrs. Gilpin, I live here!" laughed John.

"There you go again!" she scolded. "You and your practical jokes. Well, I'm not falling for it this time. You go on home now, and you can come back tomorrow."

John pleaded with his brothers and sisters to "verify his credentials," but of course, they refused. They thought it was the greatest gag of all; let's get rid of John!

"Yeah, kid, go on home!" they cried in happy unison. Fortunately, a neighbor happened to drop by about that time and spoiled everybody's fun by identifying John as a Bloomingdale.

Mrs. Gilpin courageously returned, year after year, to give part of herself to our children, caring for them, playing with them, teaching them, scolding them, loving them, so that my husband and I could have, once a year, that precious weekend of quiet togetherness.

Then one year she announced: "I'm not coming anymore."

"But why, Mrs. Gilpin?" I asked. "Have the kids been that bad?"

"The *children* have been fine," she said, indicating that they were not the ones who had been naughty. "It's just that every year I come so that you two can go off for a weekend alone, and the next year when I come back I find another baby. From now on you two just better stay home and behave yourselves!"

Mrs. Gilpin is now in heaven, baby-sitting with tiny angels, no doubt. God bless her, and all "mother's helpers" everywhere, who give their time and their selves so generously to make our lives easier.

8

Big can be beautiful

A poll conducted by three professors from the University of Michigan concluded that: "Childless couples are happier than couples with children."

I have a question: How do they know? I don't mean, how do the professors know? I mean, how do the childless couples know? Since they don't have any children, how do they know they wouldn't be happier with children? I can understand how they might *think* they are happier, and far be it from me to shatter their illusions, but how can they *know?*

I can only assume that these childless couples are basing their conclusions on a recent visit to an unruly bunch of nieces and nephews. That isn't fair. *All* nieces and nephews are unruly, as any parent knows. For every parent has had the experience of watching sons and daughters who are ordinarily gentle, quiet children, turn into instant barbarians the moment relatives come to call.

Let us imagine a typical visit of a childless aunt and uncle to a normal family. Mom and Dad are quietly reading in the living room; their children: Peggy, Annie, Timmy, and what's-his-name (after the third child, who can remember names?) are enjoying a pleasant game of Monopoly at the kitchen table. The doorbell rings. It is a surprise visit from Uncle Ted and Aunt Marian. As Mom welcomes them into the living room, we hear from the kitchen:

"You embezzled from the bank, you louse! Put back that hundred bucks!"

"I did not! You're the one who's cheating! Hanging on to Boardwalk when you know I'll never sell Park Place! MEANY, MEANY, MEANY!"

Suddenly the Monopoly board flies across the room; Peg takes out after Tim, while Annie, loyal to the feminist cause, sticks out her foot and trips her brother, who wails obscenities which curl Aunt Marian's hair. What's-his-name jumps into the brawl, and all four barbarians tear through the living room, hitting and shouting, tripping over the furniture, knocking over a lamp, and pausing only long enough to yell: "Hi! Uncle Ted and Aunt Marian! Did you bring us anything?"

Dad finally shoves his shouting brood outside "to play," but the yelling and the fighting continue until the noise reaches a decibel level so high the windows shake, and Aunt Marian frantically signals to Uncle Ted: Let's get out of here! As they depart, waving halfheartedly to their nieces and nephews, said nieces and nephews are miraculously transformed back into daughters and sons, and they all go back in the house to play a quiet game of Scrabble.

Children, as children, are really a joy and a delight to have around; it is only when they turn into nieces and nephews that they become unbearable and intolerable. Aunt Marian won't believe that, of course, but it is obvious that kids can't be that bad all the time, or Mom and Dad would have cracked up long ago . . . a conclusion which Uncle Ted undoubtedly reached anyway when he heard that what's-his-name was on the way and little Timmy wasn't even walking yet.

I question the accuracy of most polls, as I will never understand how the opinions of two hundred people can reflect those of two million. But that particular poll has to be inaccurate, and I will explain why.

The probable fallacies of that poll lie in the time element. When were the childless couples polled? Were they called on Mother's Day, or Christmas, or their birthdays, when there were no little ones around to give them a handmade pencil holder, or a crayolaed egg carton for cuff links? Or perhaps on a bitter-cold, snowy morning when there were no teenagers around to shovel their driveways or warm up their cars?

Obviously not. Judging from the results of the poll (concluding that couples prefer to be childless), they were called the day they were packing for their annual Caribbean cruise; or possibly they were polled the afternoon they purchased their His and Hers sports cars. (You won't believe this, but in the past few years I, too, have purchased a couple of luxury cars: a Cadillac for our orthodontist and a Continental for our pediatrician.)

And what about the couples *with* children? Were they called at eight o'clock at night as they were tucking their freshly bathed tiny toddlers into bed with hugs and kisses and lisping I-love-yous? Or perhaps on the day their son won the four-year-scholarship, or the evening their daughter cooked them a surprise anniversary dinner?

Of course not. They were called at eight in the morning, when Mom was frantically searching for Peggy's school sweater and Tim's gym shoes and thirty-seven cents for Annie's lunch money, and Dad had just come roaring into the house to scream that he had backed the car over what's-his-name's brand-new tricycle.

See what I mean? You have to consider the circumstances.

Actually, there is no possible way anyone can accurately poll a parent. (I cannot speak for non-parents, for to be honest, I have only very vague memories of my non-parent days.) We parents are too unpredictable to be polled. We are happy one minute and hysterical the next, depending on the degree of the current crisis.

Take me, for example. If that pollster had called here last Saturday when all our kids were home, watching the Nebraska-Oklahoma football game on TV, eating freshly popped popcorn and drinking ice-cold Cokes and unitedly cheering the Cornhuskers on to victory, I wouldn't have traded any one of them for a million dollars.

On the other hand, if they had called the next day, when Danny kicked the football through our thermoglass picture window, and Mike drove my car into the garage (not *in* the garage, *into* the garage, necessitating the repair of a fender and the replacement of an overhead door), and Tim pushed Patrick off the sun deck and split open his scalp (I won't even mention the damage to the rosebushes), I would probably have offered to sell the whole crew for a nickel.

Of course, I would have been subconsciously secure in the knowledge that nobody on earth would offer me the nickel.

A more recent survey revealed that "Families with one child are happier than familes with two or more children." So what's new about that? Our kids have been telling us that for years. Who do you suppose answered the questions in that survey? The mothers? The fathers? The kids? If the pollster questioned the kids, I'm surprised he got any positive answers at all. In twenty-three years of motherhood (and neighborhood) I have never met a kid (and I have met thousands) who didn't, at one time or another, think he would be happier as an only child, unless he *was* an only child, in which case he would claim that happiness is having lots of brothers and sisters.

Obviously, they didn't question the kids.

The fathers, perhaps? Not likely. Fathers seldom answer the home phone, because they know very well the call won't be for them. If Dad should happen to answer a survey phone call, he will do one of two things: (a) hang up, or (b) agree to anything because that's the quickest way to terminate the call. Pollsters know that fathers give very unreliable answers.

But as this particular survey claimed to be very reliable (few admit to being unreliable), I can only assume that the questions must have been put to mothers. Before we can accept absolute reliability, however, we must once again consider the time element: the hour of the day and the season of the year that mother was queried.

Ask any mother of an only child, in late afternoon, during the second week of summer vacation, if she wished she had more than one child, and she will undoubtedly proclaim: "You bet I do. I'd give anything for a live-in playmate for Buddy. If I have to lose one more game of Six Million Dollar Man, I'll go bananas."

On the other hand, if you ask that same mother that same question on a September morning when she is totaling the bills for school clothes, school supplies, gym uniform, scout dues, et cetera, she will undoubtedly reply: "Not on your life. I can't afford the one I've got."

As for the mother of many children, no pollster can get an answer out of her because no pollster can get her on the phone. It's always busy. But should one happen to contact a mother-of-many, one can count on a lengthy, detailed answer, because it's *so nice to talk to another adult for a change.* Said mother will always admit that she is content with the number of her brood . . . unless, of course, it is eight o'clock on a winter morning and the kids are ready to go off to school and this mother of ten can find only seven coats, three caps, and nine mittens, none of which match. Her answer under those circumstances? "Why didn't I become a nun?!"

Everytime I read a news story reporting that "big families are a thing of the past; there are none around today," I call up my three married sisters, with their total of seventeen children, to tell them that we don't exist. I don't know how many children it takes to constitute a "big family," but I do know that in our

Catholic parish, we, with our ten children, do not rank in the top ten among big families. I have one friend who is the mother of seventeen; another has fourteen children; more than a dozen I know have twelve; and families with ten children, in the Archdiocese of Omaha, are too numerous to count. If you are concerned about the population explosion, and dedicated to zero population, for heaven's sake don't move to Omaha. Our contentment is contagious.

There will always be big families, because there will always be parents who remember the joys of being raised in a big family, or who always envied the neighbor kids who came from a big family. They know that a big family is a happy family, and they want their own children to learn the delights and discipline, the blessings and benefits of having lots of siblings.

Just consider some of those joys and blessings:

In a big family, when one child says: "Anybody want to go outside and toss a football around?" he's got an instant team.

For the "little brother" in a big family, there is always a big brother to take you to camp-outs and games and scout meetings, and a big sister to iron on your scout badges and listen to your riddles and tease the tears away if Mama's not around.

On the other hand, if you are the "big brother" in a big family, there is always a little brother who can be bribed to run an errand for you, or a little sister who can be cajoled into taking your turn at the dishes.

Being a child in a big family means if you can't find your coat, it's okay; there's an extra one hanging in the closet. It also means not having a guilty conscience when Mom accuses: "Somebody used up all the milk last night," because you know that three of the other kids sneaked downstairs for a bowl of cereal, too.

Members of a big family never argue about where to go on their vacation because they never take a vacation.

The oldest child in a big family gets a lot of attention because his or her parents feel he was cheated out of his babyhood by the rapid arrival of younger siblings.

The youngest child in a big family gets a lot of attention because there are no more babies for everybody to fawn over.

The middle children in a big family get a lot of attention because they learn early in life *to demand it.*

The *little* kids in a big family never find it difficult to clean up their plates because by the time they get served the chicken is almost gone and they only get a little bit anyway.

The *big* kids in a big family get lots of new clothes because Mom figures she might as well make the investment; seven other kids will eventually wear them.

All the kids in a big family get plenty of privacy because everybody spies to see if anybody else is spying.

Kids in a big family always have somebody to play with and somebody to fight with, somebody to hate and somebody to love, somebody to hit and somebody to hug.

What's it like being in a big family?

It's a little like living in Nebraska. Nobody in their right mind would want to live there except those who already do, and they know that it's a delightful state to be in. Take it from one who knows, on both counts.

Part III

. . . And then the school-boy, with his satchel
And shining morning face, creeping like a snail,
Unwillingly to school . . .

SHAKESPEARE, *As You Like It*

9

Dear sirs: . . .

Remember in those Victorian novels when the lady of the house would go, each morning after breakfast, to her Morning Room to take care of her correspondence? I always used to wonder who on earth she was writing all those notes to. Now I know. She was writing to her children's teachers.

I can't remember exactly when my daily correspondence with the parochial-school teachers began, but I think it was sometime in 1960 when I wrote to explain to Reverend Mother Regan just exactly why we were enrolling our three-year-old son in preschool. The explanatory note consisted of one sentence:

"Dear Reverend Mother:

Although Lee is only three years old, we request permission to enroll him in Duchesne's Pre-School because he has three little brothers.

Sincerely, . . ."

Acceptance was immediate, and compassionate. Reverend Mother Regan was, herself, from a large family.

That first note was followed in rapid succession by letters of apology: "I'm so sorry little Lee broke the blackboard; a check for reimbursement is enclosed" . . . letters of explanation: "Please note that Lee is bringing two lunch sacks to school; one holds his lunch, the other, a clean pair of pants. I'm trying!" . . . and letters of interrogation: "Have you seen Lee's shoes?"

As the years passed, my correspondence expanded to include Lee's nine brothers and sisters and covered everything from excused absences to unexcused thefts.

"Dear Sister:

I am returning a half bottle of altar wine which our acolyte lifted from the sanctuary. The bottle is only half-full because the other half is in the acolyte. He will be back in school as soon as he stops throwing up.

Sincerely,"

"Dear Sister:

I am returning three reading books, an arithmetic workbook, two missalettes, and four library books, one of which was evidently due in April 1976. Sorry about that. I am also returning a football clearly marked 'Property of Christ the King Athletic Department.' One Christ the King athlete has been duly reprimanded.

Sincerely,"

"Dear Father Pastor:

I am returning $11 which we found in our five-year-old's pocket after Sunday Mass. It seems he rifled the collection plate. When interrogated about this, he said: 'When the man passed the basket, Daddy whispered: "I shouldn't be putting in; I should be taking out!" so . . . I took out!' Daddy has been duly reprimanded.

Sincerely, . . ."

Of course, all those notes were not written on the same day, though I have been known to write more than three notes on one morning. For example, there was the morning that Mary came downstairs and said:

"Mom! Write me a note to get me out of gym, will you? Just say I can't play volleyball because of my bad ankle."

"What bad ankle?" I asked. "You mean the one you sprained last Christmas? You've played a hundred tennis games since then; surely you can play a little volleyball."

"Yeah, I know," she said, "but the truth is I need that gym period to finish an English assignment."

I refused to write a note to the gym teacher, but I did write one to the English instructor, suggesting she keep Mary after school to finish her assignment.

Peggy also needed a note to her gym teacher.

"What's the matter with you, Peg?" I asked, somewhat concerned, because Peg loves gym and hates to miss a game.

"Oh, nothing's the matter," replied Peggy cheerfully. "I just want permission to postpone my badminton test because I lost my outline."

"Your outline?" I asked. "You mean you *study* badminton?"

"Of course," she said. "It's one of my favorite subjects."

"I bet it is," I replied sarcastically. "Do you ever study English, history, math, or science?"

"Oh sure," she said. "Every Monday and Friday. Unless, of course, there happens to be a movie scheduled then, or a field trip, or a workshop. Which reminds me, I need a field-trip permission slip for extended homeroom."

"What is 'extended homeroom'?" I asked. "Do you go to the museum or an art gallery or someplace like that?"

"Sometimes," she said. "But not often. This week we're going to the Pizza Hut for lunch. We're studying the eating habits of American teenagers." (In an hour? Good luck!)

Danny had to have a note because he had been sick the day before, and Jim had to have one because he hadn't been.

"You weren't home sick yesterday, Jim," I said. "Why do you need a note?"

" 'Cause I wasn't at school, either," he admitted. It seems that Jim and another Junior had been sent to deliver some textbooks to the neighboring girls' high school, and when they took them to the school library, ancient Sister Sapienzia invited them to the cafeteria for lemonade and cookies, and there they found the cheerleaders practicing their stunts, and well, you know how it is, Mom. I know how it is; never could trust those cheerleaders. Who'd have thought they'd come back to haunt me, thirty years later.

"How about you, Annie?" I asked. "Don't you need a note?"

"Nope," replied Annie. "I just need you to sign my math paper, so the teacher will know you helped me with it."

"But I didn't help you with it," I replied.

"I know," she said. "Jim did. The last time you helped me I got an F." I wrote a note anyway, this one suggesting that they do away with either (a) modern math, or (b) parental help.

Tim needed a note explaining that he was wearing forbidden sneakers instead of required school shoes, though I felt it was futile, for what sixty-eight-year-old nun is going to understand how a fourth-grade boy could drop his shoes down a storm sewer?

"What about you, Patrick?" I asked as I hugged my youngest. "Do you need a note?"

"No," he replied shyly, "but I do need a quarter for a new notebook."

"Patrick!" I admonished. "I just bought you a new notebook last week. How could you use up all those pages?"

"I didn't," he replied. "You just did, writing all those notes!"

I winced. Not because I begrudge Patrick the quarter, but because I knew I would have to open my billfold, and the very sight of money reminds my children of immediate and imperative needs.

"I need a nickel for a library fine," said Peggy.

"That reminds me," said Dan, "I need $1.19 for a workbook, and it's gotta be in exact change."

It is a Catholic fact of life that all fees assessed by parochial-school teachers are expected to be sent in "exact change, please." This law was introduced, undoubtedly, by the very first of a continuous line of Sister-Mary-School-Supplies who announce each morning, as the kids line up to buy erasers, notebooks, pencils, et cetera: "I am not running a bank here!"—a statement mothers have often had occasion to doubt.

We managed to find the quarter for Pat and the nickel for Peg and the dollar and nineteen cents for Dan, as well as a dime for Annie's mission box, when Pat announced:

"I need another seven cents."

"What for?" I asked.

"The class is having a party today and Sister's bringing the cake, but we each have to have seven cents for milk."

"Look, Pat," I sighed, "I have just scrounged under the sofa cushions for change; I have ripped off your father's petty-cash box; I have gone through the winter-coat pockets; I have looked under the rug. There is no more money in this house. Here, take Annie's dime; she can donate to the missions tomorrow."

"I can't take a dime," said Pat, stubbornly.

"Why not?" I asked.

"Because I have to have exact change," he repeated. "Say, I've got an idea! Why don't you write a check?"

If there is anybody who intimidates me more than nuns who demand exact change, it is bankers who frown on checks written for seven cents. I opted for the ire of the nuns, and wrote another note, this one begging to borrow seven cents until tomorrow, or at least until the store opened and I could cash a check and hand-deliver one nickel and two pennies to Patrick's class-room teacher.

After which I shall return to the store, buy a box of stationery, and write yet another note, this to the publishers of those Victorian novels, to correct their spelling.

"Dear Sirs:

"You know in those novels where your heroine retires after breakfast to her Morning Room to take care of her correspondence? That should be spelled 'M-o-u-r-n-i-n-g.'"

10

Pretty good is pretty awful

Of all the communications between parents and teachers, the most dreaded has to be the annual Letter to Parents from "The School." The Letter is sent out in late September or early October, after the kids have been in school long enough for the teachers to realize that the little angels who enrolled in September are, unfortunately, the same little devils who left school last May.

The Letter reminds parents that: Your children *must* be at school before eight-fifteen but not before eight-twelve . . . that children who live within walking distance (ten miles) *must* go home to lunch . . . that a strict dress code *must* be followed . . . that you must not request your child be assigned to another homeroom . . . et cetera, et cetera, et cetera.

After fifteen years of being told what my children *must* do, my satirical soul rebelled, and I decided to retaliate. So, working on the theory that the best defense is offense, I composed the following "Letter to Teachers from the Parent":

"To all teachers: Please put this in a prominent place on your desk so that you may refer to it throughout the year. Attach it securely, as no copies will be made available.

"So that there is no misunderstanding between thee and me, it is expected that the following rules be obeyed:

"1. Students *must* leave their homes not later than 8 A.M. and return not earlier than 3 P.M. No hanging around the front yards, please. Parents have enough to do in the mornings without baby-sitting with your students.

"2. Students may come home for lunch only if they live within thirty feet of school.

"3. If school is to be dismissed at noon on any given day, notice must be sent home thirty-six months in advance.

"4. No student may come home claiming illness unless he (a) is bleeding from both ears, (b) has a broken bone protruding from the skin, (c) is unconscious. In such cases, the student may come home if he brings a note from the school nurse testifying that the child is not faking it.

"5. Oil paints, India ink, and Magic Markers are strictly prohibited and, if brought into the home, will be confiscated and destroyed. In the event that said items are smuggled into the home, and are found by a preschool age brother or sister, it shall be understood that the teacher will then be required to report to the home that evening to wash down the walls, clean the carpets, and explain the whole mess to Dad.

"6. Requests for milk money, hot-lunch money, mission-box money, field-trip money, *any* money, must be made before the twenty-first of the month, as no respectable mother can be expected to come up with any petty cash after that date.

"7. Students who are persuaded to go out for band will be allowed to practice only in the home of the band instructor.

"8. In the interests of peace at home, the following policy will be strictly adhered to: No PTA meetings, scout banquets, Christmas programs, graduations, et cetera, may be scheduled on Monday nights unless they are first cleared with Howard Cosell.

"9. Students are expected to return home from school in reasonably reputable clothes. Trousers with holes, jackets with rips, and shoes with irremovable tar will not be tolerated. In the case of primary students, parents of first- and second-graders will be satisfied if their children just return home in the same clothes they wore to school.

"10. We realize that personality conflicts may occur throughout the year. However, we must insist that teachers do not request that their students be assigned to another family. While many parents would be happy to cooperate with such a request, surveys have shown that one home is pretty much like another, and students and teachers will just have to adjust.

"If you have any questions concerning this letter, please feel free to call me anytime before 3 P.M. yesterday afternoon.

"Most sincerely,"

Actually, I haven't written The Letter yet, but I'm going to . . . just as soon as I can find a pencil.

I don't know why parents and teachers even try to communicate; it's a waste of time, since we obviously don't speak the same language. Parents speak English, and teachers speak Teacher Talk, a special code which changes with each generation so that parents can't pass it on to their married children.

I first confronted this code when I attended Hilltop, the Convent of the Sacred Heart in St. Joseph, Missouri. The Sacred Heart nuns, gentle souls that they were, could not bear to hurt the feelings of the suffering saints who spent twice as much time with their students as they did, so they devised a method of telling parents, in diplomatic ways, that their kids were little stinkers.

This method was unfolded each week at a general assembly of students called Primes. Every Monday morning the student body would meet in the Assembly Room, where, in the presence of Reverend Mother and the entire faculty, the Mistress General would read aloud our individual conduct ratings. There were four ratings: Very Good, Good, *Pretty* Good (which, relatively speaking, obviously meant pretty *bad*), and No Notes, which nobody ever got because that meant automatic expulsion and the nuns were not about to turn us loose to the co-ed classrooms of Central High.

Since nobody ever got No Notes, the worst anybody could get was Pretty Good. The record for consistency at Primes (and as far as I know, the record still stands) was held by my friend, Mary Therese, a jolly girl who was admired by her fellow students because she once confused Mother Edwards to the point of speechlessness. (There was a rumor that she also made Mother Meyer smile, but this was never verified by witnesses and consequently has been attributed to Mary Therese's tendency to exaggerate her achievements.)

Mary Therese was consistent in that every single Monday she got *Pretty* Good at Primes. For four years we worried that Mary Therese's parents would punish her for such conduct by depriving her of the privilege of attending Hilltop and thereby depriving us of Mary Therese's entertaining antics. But Mary Therese's parents were amazingly tolerant, and it wasn't until graduation day that we discovered why. In thanking the nuns for giving his daughter such an excellent education, Mary Therese's father turned to the Mistress General and said:

"We're certainly proud of our Mary; her grades may not have been terrific but she is a fine young girl. Why, do you realize that there wasn't one single week that our Mary didn't get Pretty *Good* at Primes?"

"I certainly do realize it," sighed Mother McNally, as she diplomatically decided not to correct the emphasis.

Today's teacher's code is just as diplomatic, but it is much more complicated. When you or I attend a parent-teacher conference, we can expect to hear things like:

"Dan is an underachiever." Which means, of course, that Dan is lazy.

If they tell me that "Annie's behavior hinders her progress," I know that means Annie has been showing off again.

And when they tell me that "Patrick is more play-oriented than work-oriented," I breathe a sigh of relief. Patrick is evidently a perfectly normal, work-hating-play-loving little boy.

For the benefit of you younger parents who are yet unfamiliar with the Code, here are a few interpretations:

"Freddie does not work independently" means that good old Freddie cheats.

"Charles sometimes neglects his personal appearance" can be construed to mean that Charles has been wearing the same shirt since September, and the whole class would be grateful if you would throw it in the wash and Charlie along with it.

"Allen overemphasizes athletics" is leading up to the revelation that Allen underemphasizes English, history, math, science, et cetera.

"John loves to be outdoors" means it takes three upperclassmen and the janitor to drag Johnny in from recess.

"Little Teddy is doing fine in first grade, but he must learn to overcome his feelings of insecurity" means Little Teddy can't bring his blanket to school anymore.

"Alice fails to grasp the basic concepts of the subject matter" has only one interpretation: Alice is going to flunk.

"Harold has a questionable grasp of the basic concepts of the subject matter" does not mean the same thing, however. Actually, Harold may be just as dumb, if not dumber, than Alice, but the teacher saves herself here by changing the phrase "fails to grasp" to "a questionable grasp." She doesn't mind having sweet Alice back in her homeroom next year, but there is no way she is going to spend another nine months with that horrible Harold.

Once you learn the Code, you will have a much clearer idea of how your child is doing in school. If you want a clearer idea, that is. Personally, I prefer the old Primes ratings, for even though I know what it means, *Pretty* Good still sounds Pretty *Good* to me.

I hate parent-teacher conferences, and when I got the quarterly "invitation" to one last week, I told my husband:

"If I'm lucky, I'll break a leg, or come down with some contagious disease, or crack up and get myself committed. I'm not going to that meeting; I can't; I won't; I refuse."

"Don't be such a coward," he said. "It's just a fifteen-minute conference with the same teacher who has taught six of our older kids. You know her, she knows you, you'll get along fine."

"What do you mean: *I'll* get along fine? What about 'we'll get along fine'? Fathers are supposed to go, too, you know."

"Yeah, I know," he said, "and I really wish I could, but it just so happens I have a board meeting that morning." What a coincidence. Who's the coward?

If I had my way, parent-teacher conferences would be banned. They are so unfair. The teacher always has the advantage because she is on her own home ground, while the poor parent is the one who must stand and wait in a strange hallway (would that it *were* strange; I have stood in that hallway so often and for so long I feel as if I should pay rent), intimidated by the smell of chalk and gym shoes and the presence of other pale parents.

What's the teacher going to say to me?

The primary teachers don't bother me, because primary students are so cute neither the teacher nor the parent can find fault with them. Anyway, primary teachers all seem to be about twenty years old, and nothing boosts my self-confidence so much as being on the right side of the generation gap. When a mother reaches the age where a teacher calls her "Ma'am," all is guaranteed to go well.

The middle teachers don't bother me, either, because this year my "middle children" are girls, and girls are always good. (Comparatively speaking, of course. To a mother of seven sons, any girl looks good.)

It's the junior-high teacher who does me in. Any woman who has spent six hours a day for the last five months teaching fourteen-year-old boys has undoubtedly become a little intolerant.

Toddlers may be cute, and girls are good, but fourteen-year-old boys are, let's face it, *awful*.

But why am I so scared to face that teacher? I am not the fourteen-year-old boy. I am not the one who kicked the football through the auditorium window, nor did I accidentally (?) set off the fire alarm. And how was I to know, when my son asked permission to take his pet to school for Fun Day, that he meant his pet spider? I didn't even know he had a pet spider; I thought he meant the poodle.

I suppose I am responsible for not checking his textbooks to see if he had defaced them by scribbling in the margin, but I do think she got a little upset over one French word! Anyway, how was I to know what it meant? I have enough trouble cleaning up one language. Why do they have to teach him two?

As I approached the junior-high homeroom in panicky anticipation of the forthcoming conference, I suddenly wondered if possibly the teacher dreaded this conference as much as I did.

Evidently she did. She wasn't there. There was a note on the door:

"To the parents of junior-high students: Teacher will not be here today; she broke her leg."

I bet she did. She should have claimed: ". . . cracked up and committed." That I would have believed.

I always blanch when the kids come home from school and tell me that their teacher is "Miss" Somebody. With four kids graduated, and six currently in school, we have benefited from a variety of teachers: Fathers (Jesuits and diocesan priests); fathers (married), bachelors, nuns, ex-nuns, Mrs., Ms., and Misses. But it is "Miss" who will be the death of me, for she is always the one who sends home a note commanding that my child return to school the next morning with a cigar box, or three feet of clothesline, or six yards of magenta-colored material. How do you tell an eight-year-old child that Mama doesn't even know what color magenta is?

Men teachers don't bother with such things. It's not that they are above all things artistic, it's just that they think it's more important to emphasize reading, writing, and 'rithmetic because if a little boy doesn't learn the basics, the principal won't let him play on the football team.

Mrs. Teacher understands that mothers are too busy to be scrounging around for such articles at eight in the morning; Ms. Teacher is convinced that Mother is too stupid to send the right materials, anyway; while Sister Teacher (bless her!) has anything and everything she will ever need for any project stashed in the back of the convent closet. (In the old days, when the nuns wore long, black habits, Sister stashed everything in those deep, delightfully mysterious pockets.)

But Miss Teacher is still young and enthusiastic, talented and trusting, and is determined to teach the children to make lovely jewelry boxes (for all those jewels Mama has been wondering what to do with) out of a cigar box and $18 worth of glitter and ribbon.

Have you ever tried to buy an empty cigar box? Don't; there aren't any. True, cigars still come in boxes; but it seems if you want the box, you have to buy all the cigars. This may seem a little extravagant, especially if you are a non-smoker, but the reader must remember that teachers in Catholic schools always assume that all families should have frequent occasion to pass out cigars.

Even less available than empty cigar boxes are short pieces of clothesline. If, on the off-chance you find a store that still sells clothesline, you can be sure that the clerk will not agree to cutting you off a three-foot piece. You must buy the whole length, which you will then take home and hide in the basement in the hopes that your husband won't find it and suggest you string it across the backyard and make use of it. (Also, there may be times when you are tempted to throw it over the basement rafter and suggest *he* make use of it.) Better just to cut your three-foot piece and throw the rest away.

Actually, a cigar box and clothesline will probably be the most practical things you are asked to send to school. I remember one week I was asked to send a spool of purple thread, a carpet needle, a size-twelve shoe box, and twenty-four multicolored turkey feathers. Where is an old city gal like me supposed to find turkey feathers? I'll tell you where: in a Specialty Shop, for $1.98 a feather.

It is not just finding the materials that takes time and talent, what really takes talent is to show surprise and delight when, a week after buying the above-listed materials, your kid comes home with a size-twelve "turkey." You may be able to express delight for a few minutes, but how about next week? And the next? For you can be sure that Mr. Turkey is going to be around for a while.

What do parents do with all the things their kids bring home from school? I know some devoted and dedicated parents keep every single thing their children create, but with ten children, each producing things in kindergarten, cub scouts, blue birds, craft classes . . . not to mention the weapons my teenagers made in shop class . . . it could get a little crowded.

So, God forgive me, I throw those things away, but only after a suitable period of veneration, of course.

If you are going to follow my example, however, I must warn you to be discreet. After having paid due respect to that size-twelve turkey, which served as a centerpiece for Thanksgiving and again for Christmas, I slipped it into the trash can and put it on the curb to await the sanitation pick-up.

Thirty minutes later, Tim came rushing in, shouting triumphantly:

"Boy, Mom, are you lucky! Look what somebody accidentally threw away!"

That year we had a most unique centerpiece for Easter dinner. But by that time the features were so frayed, it really did look a little like a size-twelve bunny.

11

Where does it hurt?

Modern medicine has made another magnificent discovery. After years of research, laboratory studies, X rays, conferences, and listening to little kids' complaints, medical men agree that the school child's 8 A.M. tummy ache, which disappears as the school bus turns the corner, is indeed the real thing.

I knew that. I can remember that "afraid-to-go-to-school stomachache." In fact, I still get it, not because I am afraid to go to school, but because each morning at eight I am afraid one or more of the kids won't go to school.

I always make it a point to listen to my children's aches and pains because I have always harbored a hatred for people who wouldn't listen to mine. Like my obstetrician. Every time I got pregnant my obstetrician would tell me sternly:

"There is no such thing as morning sickness. It is all in your head."

I should have put it all in his lap.

Then there were the labor pains. For thousands of years mothers were glorified and sanctified for enduring the horrors of labor pains, until my turn came. That was the year the American Medical Association announced: "There are no such things as labor pains; contractions would be painless if mothers would just learn to relax."

Relax, he says. Here you are, Mother, lying flat on a clammy, cold delivery table, with your arms and legs strapped down so you can't even scratch your nose or wiggle your toes; you haven't eaten since last night and you sure wouldn't have had three helpings of spaghetti if you'd known the nurses would insist on draining it all out of you, and . . . My God, the spaghetti; did you leave it on the burner? And you are supposed to relax?

Of course contractions don't hurt! Why should they? What's painful about an eight-pound place-kicker practicing punts when he's supposed to be putting in an appearance?

I have a question, Doctor. How many members of the American Medical Association have ever experienced labor?

I shouldn't really blame it all on obstetricians; psychiatrists are just as bad. I ran into a psychiatrist friend of mine the other day and when he saw I was wearing a copper bracelet he said:

"Aha, I see you think you have arthritis."

I am not even going to be allowed to suffer in my old age. A recent medical report indicated that: "Senility is psychosomatic and can be conquered by activity." Now there's a plot made up by somebody's kids. I can see my children now, *circa* 1999, hiding my rocking chair and handing me a scrub mop. "Got to keep active, Grandma! You just *think* you're old!"

I wouldn't be surprised if, when the time comes for me to be wheeled into Westside Chapel, the mortician would smile down upon me and say: "Ah, Teresa, I see you think you're dead."

Please don't let that happen. If I'm going to have to spend a lifetime trying to convince some doctor I hurt, I am certainly not going to spend eternity trying to tell a mortician I'm dead. Just let me rest in peace.

If I have been hard on the medical profession, I beg to exclude from my excoriations all pediatricians, those saintly souls who devote their lives to consoling nervous mothers, tuning out frantic fathers, and lovingly caring for squalling infants who invariably thank the doctor for the exam or shot by spraying him right in the eye.

Pity the poor pediatrician! Half the adult population (the male half) condemn him, not only for his wisdom and his wealth, but also for his inaccessibility at four o'clock on Saturday afternoon when Mom is out shopping and Dad is baby-sitting and the baby has been screaming for six and a half innings straight.

The female half of the population lives in tembling awe of the pediatrician, fearful that he will claim that Baby's sniffles or scratches are due to Mother's incompetence or negligence, and he will "take the baby back." I know it's crazy, but every mother feels that part of her baby belongs to the pediatrician, and he reserves the right to revoke her maternity. I had been going to the same pediatrician for years before I realized that the last thing in the world he would do would be to lay claim to one of my kids.

Children alternate between loving and hating their pediatrician, depending on whether he is passing out lollipops or inoculations.

I miss my pediatrician. We met regularly for years, but I seldom see him anymore, not because I ran out of kids, but because I ran out of money. With the first five children, I was faithful about regular check-ups, examinations, and inoculations, but the second five have to get sick before they get to see a doctor, and then the problem is usually resolved by a phone call. I have become such an expert at diagnosing, he can now prescribe by long distance. Consequently, I now see him only once or twice a year for something really serious.

Such was certainly not always the case. In the "good old days" it was not unusual for my pediatrician and me to meet twice, or even three times, in the same day.

I recall one time, when Lee was about ten years old, and he sailed off down the street on his bike, turned too quickly into a neighbor's driveway and crashed into the neighbor's new car, doing considerable damage to the left-rear fender. He also did considerable damage to his own right knee, which as any lawyer's child will tell you, is not nearly as serious as banging up the neighbor's car, especially if the neighbor also happens to be a lawyer.

I had just returned from the pediatrician's office where I had taken our two-year-old Danny for a measles inoculation, so I knew the doctor was in his office. I called him immediately, and when I described the accident, he told me to take the injured child to the hospital and he would meet us there. He then gave up his lunch hour to come to the hospital, where he examined my son, ordered X rays, and recommended an overnight stay.

While we were at the hospital, the baby-sitter called to tell me that she had gone outside to look for the four-year-old and as soon as she stepped outside, the six-year-old had slammed and locked the door, leaving her outside and himself inside, happily plotting mischief with his brother.

I hurried home to find that another of my sons, on returning home from baseball practice, had "come to the rescue" by breaking a window to gain entry and, in so doing, slashed open his hand.

So it was back to the pediatrician's office for stitches. While the doctor was sewing up the hand, his own wife called to ask him to come home as she had just gone into labor. Without missing a stitch, the doctor ordered his nurse to dismiss his patients, lock up his office, and tell his wife he would be right there . . . as soon as he finished with the Bloomingdales. Do you see why I'm devoted to that doctor? What a marvelous man! (If I'd been his wife, I would have killed him.)

I then hurried home, got dinner on the table, and accompanied my husband back to the hospital to check on our other injured son, who was thoroughly enjoying himself, sipping 7-Up, watching TV, and pestering all the nurses.

When I came home at nine o'clock to put the kids to bed, I undressed our Danny and discovered he was covered from shoulder to toe with a terrible rash; he had overreacted to the measles shot. Was it serious? I had no choice but to call the doctor, who evidently decided that my bad day had been worse than his bad day, because he made a house call to put my mind at ease.

The other day I happened to pass by that pediatrician's office, and as I listened to the squalling infants and tearful toddlers, I could not help but think once again: Pity the poor pediatrician. My babies are finally growing up, but his will stay infants forever.

My love affair with the children's doctor does not extend to their dentist. I know, God told us we must love one another, but . . . surely He didn't mean *dentists!* For years I managed to stay neutral about dentists, for the simple reason that I never went to one. When the kids get cavities or need check-ups or braces, I drive them to the dentist, drop them off, and return to pick them up. That way I don't have to listen to them scream, and the dentist doesn't have to listen to me demanding to know why they are screaming.

Last year I met the children's dentist for the first time face to face, or mouth to fist, to be more precise. I had broken a tooth and after a couple of days of discomfort I concluded that I must either go to the dentist or let my tongue be slowly sliced away. (The kids were hoping I'd opt for the latter.)

I hadn't been to a dentist in years, so I was unprepared for that tortuous invention called the rubber dam. (More appropriate to call it, I would think, the rubber *damn.*) A rubber dam is a hot, slimy, ghastly mask which the dentist nails to your face with the excuse that it will isolate the work area. Actually, the real purpose of this horror is to make it impossible for the patient to cry out in pain, or to make caustic comments while the dentist drills through your jawbone.

Since the dentist's time is very valuable, his dental assistant attaches the rubber dam, and generally prepares you for the work to be done. As soon as the monstrous mouthpiece is attached, the assistant disappears, supposedly to summon the dentist. In fact, they both go out to lunch.

Meanwhile, you are left gagged, unable to breathe, speak or swallow. Your sinuses begin to drain, and just about the time you resign yourself to a death brought on by an inability to either swallow or spit, the dentist will pop back into view with a cheerful greeting and a set of tools he borrowed from the guy who is outside breaking up the street.

There are two kinds of dentists: those who carry on a running conversation with the nurse, causing you to wonder if they are paying enough attention to your teeth, and those who peer silently into your mouth and never utter a word except an occasional "Open!" "Shut!" and "Oops!"

Dentists, like plasterers, paper-hangers, and teenage sons, work awhile and then wander off.

"Got to let that set a minute," the dentist will say as he dashes into the next room to pick up another fifty bucks, and you will sit there looking frantically through your eyebrows, watching for his return.

You will hear him laughing and chatting in the next room, and his good humor will grate on your nerves. An hour in the dentist's chair is a miserable experience, and the least the dentist can do is respect your rotten mood. Laughing, joking, and cheerful chatting should be forbidden. I especially hate it when the dentist has greeted me with an obvious lie: "Hi! Teresa, you're looking marvelous. Sit down here and relax; this won't hurt a bit."

I would feel much better about the whole thing if he would snarl:

"Only an idiot would eat Cracker Jacks at your age. Hang on, because this will blow you right out of the chair!"

I mean, since you are going to hate the dentist anyway, the least he can do is be hateable.

12

Thou shalt not put peanut butter in the refrigerator. . . .

My neighbor, Nancy, dropped in for a cup of coffee the other day and I had to give it to her in a jelly glass because all the mugs were either in the TV room, on the garage roof (please don't ask me to explain that), or under Danny's bed.

"I see your kids are just like mine," said Nancy as she stirred her coffee with a fork. "Last night our Joe ground up two spoons in the garbage disposal, just after he had broken the tip off my best paring knife, prying the lid off a jar of olives."

"It isn't their absentmindedness that bothers me," I commiserated with her. "It is their stupidity. Just this morning I went to pack the school lunches and I found the peanut butter in the refrigerator, the bananas in the freezer, and the potato chips in Peggy. Now nobody, *nobody*, not even the dumbest kid in the world, puts peanut butter in the refrigerator. And of course I am supposed to believe that 'nobody put it there.' It evidently came factory-installed."

I don't know what they teach kids in school these days, but I think they'd be wise to forget about compulsory phys. ed. and concentrate on a course in common sense. They could start with simple lessons like:

"We do not put peanut butter in the refrigerator because this makes peanut butter hard and impossible to spread and that makes Mother nervous and impossible to live with."

Or: "We do not drink the last of the orange juice with our midnight snack, when we know that our dad likes orange juice with his breakfast."

I can think of a whole list of commandments which should be memorized by all children over the age of five. For example:

1. It shall be strictly forbidden for anyone to put an empty milk carton into the refrigerator or an empty ice tray into the freezer.

2. Clothes to be thrown down the clothes chute or into the clothes hamper must first be removed from the hanger.

3. Mother's manicure scissors must never be used to cut the tops off cereal boxes. Nor may the boxtops be cut off before the cereal is all gone, at which time, and only then, is it permissible to remove the premium toy from the bottom of the box. Under no circumstances may the cereal be poured into the sink to find the premium. The premium toy automatically becomes the property of the youngest child in the household, unless it sticks, pokes, scratches, or leaves an indelible mark, in which case it is to be surreptitiously destroyed. (The toy, not the child.)

4. We do not put bananas in the freezer; we do not put banana peels in the piano bench.

5. It is considered inexpedient for a teenage son to go off on a weekend camp-out with both sets of Dad's car keys in his pocket.

6. Under no circumstances may our home be shared with the following: (a) a bird whose wing the cat just chewed off; (b) any pet remotely resembling a rodent; (c) anything at all that is offensively odoriferous. (Exceptions will be made, however reluctantly, if the odoriferous object is a twelve-year-old boy who belongs here.)

7. Teaspoons, cereal bowls, coffee cups, Coke glasses, et cet-

era, when removed from the kitchen, must be returned to said kitchen within a reasonable period of time. (Like less than three months.)

8. Teenagers who are fortunate enough to own their own stereos shall not tune them to be heard in the next county; nor may two or more teenagers in the same household play their stereos simultaneously; nor may they play them after 11 P.M., nor may they play them at all if Mother happens to have her stereo tuned to Frank Sinatra.

9. It should be understood that, when Mother says: "Take those filthy tennis shoes down to the laundry room and put them in the washing machine right this very minute!" she should not be taken literally if, at right this very minute, her Irish lace tablecloth is in the rinse cycle.

10. Teenagers who are asked by Dad to: "Put the car away for me, will you, son?" shall do so without (a) turning the radio to full volume and leaving it there, (b) filling the ashtrays with cigarette stubs, gum wrappers, or both, (c) using more than half a tank of gas.

When they read the above commandments for kids, my children demanded the right to rebuttal and submitted the following commandments for parents:

(1) Thou shalt not, if the weather turns suddenly cold on a school day, bring my jacket to school and say to the teacher in front of the whole third grade: "Will you give this to Sonny Boy? I wouldn't want him to catch cold."

(2) Thou shalt not, if I am on a date with the cutest boy in the senior class, leave the porch light burning.

(3) Thou shalt not, when we are entertaining friends, show off the family album, the family trophies, or the family parents.

(4) Thou shalt not, when I am studying at the kitchen table with my steady girl friend, Sally, ask: "Would you like another cup of coffee, Linda?" (Linda's long gone, Mother; try to keep current!)

(5) Thou shalt not, when chaperoning our school dances, dance. (For heaven's sake, Dad, nobody *dips* anymore.)

(6) Thou shalt not, even in the privacy of our own home, refer to any of us as: Honey; Sweetie; Precious; Sonny Boy; Baby; Sugar, unless one of us is still under the age of two, which, considering Mom's age, is not likely. (Let us hope!)

(7) Thou shalt not, when entering our bedrooms, ask any of the following questions:

"What's that I smell?"

"How can you live in this pigpen?"

"Are you going to sleep all week?"

"What's that magazine you just shoved under your mattress?"

(On second thought, how about: "Thou shalt not enter our bedrooms . . . period?")

(8) Thou shalt not go out to dinner on Saturday night with both sets of car keys in thy purse.

(9) Thou shalt not let thy gasoline credit cards expire.

(10) Thou shalt always be available to: cook meals; lend money; help with homework; listen to worries and woes; love us as much as we love you.

How could kids who make that much sense put peanut butter in the refrigerator?

They couldn't, of course. Not my perfect children. So it must have been Kilroy.

World War II veterans have been wondering for years what happened to Kilroy, the mischievous little gremlin who went about the war wreaking havoc, raising tempers, taunting and teasing, but never getting caught. I can now tell you where Kilroy is. At our house.

Kilroy came to live with us over twenty years ago. He didn't ask permission, or introduce himself, he just sneaked in and made himself at home. I never saw him, but I knew he was there because he left illegible messages, scribbled with crayon, on the nursery walls. He would also hide the baby's booties, and steal the toddler's mittens and caps, and when the children went to sleep at night, he would hide their shoes in the sandbox or shove them under the sofa. Then, before retiring himself, Kilroy would make one final attempt to get my toddlers in trouble by carefully placing their trikes in the driveway, directly behind their father's car.

As our children grew older, Kilroy became more sophisticated in his taunts. Instead of hiding shoes under the sofa, he would stuff pop bottles under there, along with one or two pieces of Dad's chess set, my reading glasses, and a couple of pages out of *Playboy,* which, needless to say, he stole from some neighbor.

Kilroy's favorite haunt is the kitchen, where, late at night, he broils bacon and brews coffee, makes pizza or peanut-butter sandwiches, puts empty cereal boxes into the pantry and empty ice trays into the freezer, spills sticky substances all over the floor, and leaves the whole mess for Mother, who invariably and unjustifiably blames it all on the children.

As the years went by, Kilroy stopped scribbling on the nursery walls. Now he scribbles on the kitchen walls: telephone numbers, illegible messages for Mother, too-legible swear words for brother. The pop bottles under the sofa gave way to beer cans and cigarette stubs, most annoying to my teenage children who "never drink or smoke."

Kilroy spends an incredible amount of time in the bathroom, where he uses up all the hot water, jams my husband's razor, misplaces the comb and brush, and tosses wet towels all over the floor.

Mornings are a bad time for Kilroy; he gets particularly naughty during breakfast. While the family are gathered together at the kitchen table, Kilroy dashes upstairs to unmake the beds the kids swear they made before they came downstairs. He also dries out their toothbrushes, throws their clean clothes in the hamper and their dirty clothes in the closet, turns on all their radios, then sneaks back downstairs to hide their homework, schoolbooks, and hot-lunch money.

In recent years, Kilroy has moved out into the garage, where he spends his time siphoning gas out of my car and moving the odometer ahead so that I will accuse my "innocent" teenagers of taking my car without my permission. He even had the audacity on one occasion to forge a traffic ticket and hide it in my son's billfold. (I do not ordinarily snoop in my sons' billfolds; I was looking for a credit card which someone . . . obviously Kilroy . . . had borrowed and forgotten to return.) Incidentally, Kilroy is such an expert forger, my son agreed that it would be expedient for him to appear in court and pay Kilroy's fine. Mothers may believe in gremlins, but few judges do.

Strange as it may sound, over the past two decades I have not only adjusted to Kilroy, I have even learned to love him, and should he ever marry and move away, I know I will miss him terribly.

I just had a horrible thought: What girl in her right mind would marry a gremlin?

13

I think I forgot

When we called my parents to tell them of the birth of our fourth child, my father asked: "Don't tell me you finally have a daughter?"

"What's a daughter?" I said with a laugh. "No, Dad, it's another boy."

He roared with delight: "Serves you right, sweetheart!"

"What's that supposed to mean?" I asked.

"You were boy crazy for the first twenty-five years of your life, and those boys will drive you crazy for the next twenty-five!"

The "next twenty-five" are almost over, and those boys haven't driven me crazy yet, even though they swelled their ranks by praying for, and getting, three little brothers. Perhaps their three sisters have kept me sane, or perhaps I have managed to stay sane by staying boy crazy. I love the little jerks. I even love the big jerks. Though I'll be the first to admit that they have many faults, not the least of which is Adolescent Amnesia.

Have you ever sent a preteen or teenage boy on an errand and had him remember what he was sent for? Providing, of course, that he remembers to go in the first place.

This is not true of very little boys. Mommy can tell her three-year-old to "run upstairs and get a diaper for the baby," and her toddler will dash to the nursery and back in record time, clean diaper in hand with maybe an extra for "just in case."

Even as old as six, a little boy retains his memory. Given a message from his first-grade teacher, Junior will clutch it in his tight little fist all the way home, where he will present it proudly and promptly to Mom with orders to "read it right now!" (This explains why schools always entrust "messages to be sent home" to the youngest child in the family.)

It is sometime in the summer between first and second grade that every little boy becomes absentminded. Give a second-grader a message for Mom, and teacher will inevitably find it later, on the classroom floor, or in the lunchroom or the lavatory, or sailing through the air in the form of a well-directed spitball.

At home, little boys are even less responsible. Ask a ten-year-old to run upstairs and get a diaper for the baby, and he will say: "Sure, Mom!" and skip through the dining room, the living room, and right out the front door.

It gets worse as they get older. I have sent a sixteen-year-old to the basement to fetch me a bucket, only to have him disappear into the depths of the earth, not to surface again till suppertime.

On one occasion I sent my son Mike, then about seventeen, to my bedroom to get me a book. When he didn't come back down, I sent sixteen-year-old Jim to find him. When neither of them returned, I asked twelve-year-old Dan to go see where everybody went. A few minutes later I gave up and went upstairs to get the book myself, only to find Mike stretched out on my bed talking on my telephone; Jim, with his ear to the door, absorbing the conversation; and Danny standing on the landing, trying to remember if he was going up or coming down.

One hesitates to let such mental incompetents leave the house, but occasionally it becomes necessary to send a child to the grocery store. Unfortunately, I no longer have any sons young enough to be responsible, so I am forced to send an older boy. Here are a couple of hints from the mother of seven absent-minded sons:

Never send your son to the grocery store without making a list of items you want him to buy. This way, when he calls from the grocery store to tell you he forgot the list, you will have it readily available to read to him. (This is presuming that he remembers to go to the store, which store to go to, and the way to get there.) When he calls, you can also remind him that he didn't take the money, but to wait right there, you will send it along with his brother. When sending the second child, be sure to give him a complete description of the store, the route he is to take, and the brother he is to locate. Do not, under any circumstances, give either child cash. Always write a check; that way, you won't be so upset when they both return home, empty-handed, to tell you they lost it. Next time, send their sister.

If you must send your son on an errand, never allow him to take (a) your car, or (b) your credit card.

Last week I sent Jim to our Village Shopping Center to buy me a meat thermometer. The Village is approximately ten blocks from our house, certainly too far for a track star to travel by foot, or even by ten-speed bike. After all, he had to return carrying a three-inch thermometer. So he took the car, and, since I was out of checks (it goes without saying that I was out of cash), I gave him a credit card.

Three hours later he returned (long blocks, Mother) with a pair of jeans, a jacket, an Art Garfunkel album, and half a dozen chocolate-covered doughnuts, all charged on my credit card. He forgot the meat thermometer.

I hate to tell you this (let's hope the Russians never find out), but last summer that same son joined the United States Marine Corps. If they ever send him from the Halls of Montezuma to the Shores of Tripoli, they'd better give him a road map, a compass, and his little sister to lead the way.

Someone once wrote that the worst age for a boy is twelve. That may be the worst age for the boy, but it's the best age for his mother. Just think about it:

If, for example, Mother inadvertently throws something away on a Tuesday and doesn't realize it until Friday, she doesn't have to worry; it is still right there in the wastebasket her twelve-year-old hasn't emptied since Sunday.

Unlike his teenage brother, a twelve-year-old boy doesn't spend forty-five minutes in the shower, using up all the hot water. In fact, unless it's suggested, he won't use *any* water.

And unlike his little brother, a twelve-year-old won't wear holes in the trousers you just bought him last Tuesday, because he outgrew them on Wednesday.

A twelve-year-old boy never argues with his brother about closet space or who gets which bureau drawers, because all his clothes, books, and possessions are stuffed under his bed.

Mother never has to worry about her twelve-year-old son hanging around the drugstore after school, because she knows he is hanging around his classroom, making up an assignment he forgot to do yesterday.

Twelve is a perfect age for a boy. He is too old to need a baby-sitter, but old enough to baby-sit his younger brother or sister.

He is old enough to shovel the snow, mow the lawn, and run to the grocery store, but too young to borrow your car, your razor, or your money.

Twelve is a joy to buy gifts for, because he wants, needs, and appreciates anything and everything.

He is young enough to appreciate a one-dollar bill, but old enough to earn it himself.

He is old enough to appreciate a ten-speed bike, and young enough to think it's neater than a car.

Twelve is too old to be waited on, but too young to be waited up for.

He is too old to cling to Mom, yet still too young to criticize her.

A twelve-year-old boy has outgrown the desire to tease and taunt the girls in his class but has not yet ingrown the desire to date them.

At twelve, he is still young enough to enjoy a game of Monopoly or Scrabble, but old enough to keep track of the pieces.

Twelve is an ideal age, for the mind has at last opened up to the wonders of the world, but it cannot yet conceive the worries.

Twelve has only one fault: the inevitable turning to thirteen, when (God help us) he will become an eighth-grader, infallible, egomaniacal, and girl crazy.

Poor kid; little does he know, but he's going to be girl crazy for the rest of his life.

Part IV

. . . of shoes, and ships, and sealing wax
and cabbages, and kings . . .

LEWIS CARROLL,
"The Walrus and the Carpenter," *Through the Looking Glass*

14

Money was never meant for mothers

Until I entered high school and read my first Shakespearean play, I thought my mother had made up the phrase, "Beware the Ides of March," and I somehow associated the "ides" we were to beware with my father. For, as you remember, the ides of March meant income-tax time, and it was my mother's job to gather all the canceled checks, produce the receipts for possible deductions, and somehow explain the whole confusing mess to my father.

Having spent all those years listening to my mother bewaring the ides of March, you would think I would have had better sense than to marry the ides of April. For now, of course, income-tax time is April 15 (giving us just another month to fret and figure), and it is my job to gather the checks and do the explaining to my husband, who is affected by the ides of April in much the same manner as Lon Chaney was affected by a full moon.

When I chose a husband, I chose very carefully. Realizing that mathematics is my weak suit (actually, I am void), I decided that if I was to survive in this money-run world I would have to rely on someone else to not only make the money, but manage it as well. After much seeking and searching I finally found the perfect mate: a lawyer with a combined degree in business. It wasn't until after the wedding ceremony that he admitted to a terrible affliction: he was allergic to bills, bankbooks, and budgets.

What to do? After several months of mismanagement, we finally came to an agreement: he would make the money, and I would spend it. Idiot that I am, I thought this would be wonderful. I didn't understand the law of the land, which is: "He who makes the money must report to the IRS, and She who spends the money must report to Dracula."

The reporting is not so difficult; it's the remembering that defeats me.

First I have to remember where I put the canceled checks. In the desk? No, that's where I keep the report cards, kindergarten crafts, broken crayons, and bills which I intend to pay when their turn comes.

In the buffet? Not likely. We haven't been able to open the buffet since somebody put a ten-inch box in an eight-inch drawer back in '76.

In the sewing box? Nope, that's full of snapshots. (The needles and thread are in my jewelry box; I felt I had to keep *something* there.)

Aha, here they are, on top of the refrigerator, behind the basketball. (Note to the reader: Do not criticize unless you can tell me, right now, where *your* canceled checks are? For that matter, where is your basketball?)

Second, I have to remember what all these checks are for, like the doctor's. Let's see: there was Danny's broken arm, and Tim's earache, and Jim's strained muscle, and Annie's stitches, and Patrick's buffalo nickel. . . .

"I'm afraid to ask," interrupted my husband, "but what does Patrick's buffalo nickel have to do with the doctor?"

"Don't you remember? We had to take Pat to the doctor because he swallowed a nickel. I wouldn't have bothered for just any nickel but a buffalo nickel is rather rare. . . ."

"Okay, okay," he said, "let's go on. What's next? Ah, I had no idea we had contributed so much to the Church."

"Well, they weren't exactly *church* contributions," I admitted, "unless you can count donations to the parochial school."

"What donations?" he asked. "Did we have a fund-raiser this year?"

"We sure did," I said. "I raised funds for hot lunch, gym uniforms, library fines, scout dues, and a multitude of school supplies."

"That won't do," he said. "Didn't we contribute anything to the Church?"

"Well there was $435 for votive candles," I said.

"How in the name of heaven did we spend $435 on votive candles?" he roared.

"Actually it was only one votive candle," I admitted. "Patrick lit it, then dropped it, and set fire to the church carpet. I thought $435 was very reasonable for the amount of repairs they had to do."

"Anything else?" he sighed.

"Yes," I reported. "We gave Father $25 to repair the book rack after Jim stumbled over it, trying to get out of church quickly, and $60 to sand-blast the hopscotch pattern Peggy and Annie drew on the parking lot; then there was $14 to replace the raffle tickets Timmy lost, and another $20 I felt I had to donate to the church bazaar after I found out Danny won a radio by cheating at bingo."

"No wonder Father looks at me oddly when I drop my church envelope in the basket," said my husband. "I'm not donating to the church; I'm *buying* it."

The medical and church deductions are a simple matter; what is difficult to explain are checks written to Who Knows?

The Who Knows are the strange names which appear on

checks which I wrote but forgot to enter on my stubs, like the one written last May 18 to John Ducklesby.

"Who is John Ducklesby and why did you pay him $5.00?" asked my husband.

How am I supposed to remember who John Ducklesby is? The trash man? A repairman? A wandering minstrel? Unfortunately, I remembered.

"Never mind," I told my husband. "The $5.00 wasn't deductible."

"How do you know?" asked the accountant. "The IRS allows all kinds of deductions for seemingly ridiculous things. What was it for? Who is John Ducklesby?"

"Welllll"—I hesitated—"If you must know, he's a bookie."

"A bookie!" screamed my lawyer. "You mean our sons have been playing the horses! I'll have their hides! Which one bet the money?"

"This one," I mumbled. "I placed the bet."

"You're kidding!" he cried. "You bet on a horse? With whom?"

"John Ducklesby, obviously," I confessed. "Actually, it was through Aggie. You know Agnes; we work together at church. Well, we were putting magazines in the book rack and she told me about this sure thing at Ak-sar-ben and I wouldn't even have to go 'cause her neighbor was going and he would be happy to place the bet for me, only it wasn't such a sure thing after all and I lost the $5.00."

"You made the bet in church?" he asked.

"Yes," I admitted. "Right there in the nave, before God and everybody."

"I wonder if that could be considered a donation. . . ." pondered Dracula.

I never did ask if he claimed it as a deduction; if there is anybody I don't want to get involved with, it's the IRS. I have had only one direct confrontation with the IRS, and one was enough.

I managed to avoid direct contact with the Internal Revenue Service for twenty happily married, unemployed years, until Jo came into my life, dragging the government behind her.

The IRS would classify Jo as "domestic help," but what do they know? A woman who is courageous enough to come to my house once a week to scrape bubble gum off the oven, shovel toys out of the living room, and drag dirty socks out from under little boys' beds can hardly be called just a "cleaning lady." She ranks someplace between an angel and a saint, and since she was most certainly heaven-sent by God himself (it took three novenas and six votive candles to get her here), I don't see why I should report her presence to the United States Government, or more important, pay them for the privilege of having her around.

But of course I do pay them, since the alternative seems to be jail. I really wouldn't mind paying social security taxes, if that was all it meant—sending off a quarterly check to Washington, D.C. But anybody who has ever had domestic help, or even a saint with a shovel, knows it isn't that simple.

In the first place, the IRS isn't in Washington, D.C. It's in Ogden, Utah.

In the second place, the check must be accompanied by a printed form, but you don't have to write to Ogden, Utah, to order the form; you can get it right in your own hometown simply by calling the local office of the IRS.

Just try it.

Have you ever looked up the telephone listing for the IRS? It is not under "I," "R," or "S." It is under "U," for United States Government offices, along with 99 million other government numbers.

To make it easy for you, there is a special number for "requesting forms." But don't bother to call it, for all you get is a recording saying: "If you are requesting forms to file for employment taxes, you must call Taxes."

Okay; and what is the number for Taxes? They don't give it

to you, so you must look it up. Not under "T," dummy. Why would you look under "T"? Taxes is listed under "I." Don't ask me why. And for heaven's sake, don't ask *them* why. They will just tell you to call Information . . . which is listed under "U."

Taxes told me, when I finally got them on the phone, that they would be happy to send me the necessary forms if I would just give them my Employer Identification Number.

I told Taxes I have a social security number, a telephone number, a house number, a continuing outpatient number at Childrens Hospital's Emergency Ward, and a retired-in-my-honor number at Bergan Hospital's Maternity Ward, but those would not do. I got a new number, which I immediately memorized so I wouldn't have to look it up every time I file Jo's social security return.

When I finally received the necessary tax forms, I carefully counted the days Jo had worked for me; figured her salary; multiplied by 11.7 percent; filled out the forms, made out the check, and mailed the whole mess off to Ogden, Utah.

Two weeks later it came back. I had neglected to put Jo's identification number on the form. I had to call her to ask what her social security number was.

Have you ever tried to call your cleaning lady during the week? You can't find her. It would be easier to locate the Secretary of State. You know where she works on Monday, but this happens to be the week she traded Monday with her Tuesday lady, only she's not at her Tuesday lady's; she has been loaned to Tuesday lady's sister-in-law to help prepare for a party someplace; Tuesday lady is not too sure where.

I finally found Jo, on Thursday, when she walked in my front door. I got her SS number, remailed the file, and hoped to heaven the check wouldn't bounce.

A month later a terrible tornado hit Omaha and our house no longer needed to be cleaned because it was no longer there. Jo and I tearfully parted company and my family moved into temporary housing until we could find a new home.

Three months later, the IRS sent me another form to file the quarterly return for domestic help. Since I had no domestic help, I threw the form away.

Two weeks later they sent me a reminder. I threw *it* away.

The following week they sent me a "final notice," only, like all "final" notices, it wasn't. Several days later I received a final "final notice" in the form of a long distance telephone call asking me why I had not filed the form.

I explained that I did not file the form for domestic help because I did not have domestic help.

She replied: "Oh. In that case I will send you the form you must file when you do *not* have domestic help."

I couldn't believe it.

"That is ridiculous!" I screamed. "I do not notify the Board of Health whenever nobody has the measles! I do not notify the Bureau of Vital Statistics whenever nobody dies! I refuse to notify you when nobody works! You are all idiots down there; you are obsessed with forms, forms, forms! I hope you all strangle on your own red tape!"

And that was that!

At least that was that for that quarter. Three months later we were settled in a new home, Jo had come back to work, and my husband reminded me that I must resume paying her social security tax. But of course I had no forms, and I had forgotten the number to call. Which meant I must get out the telephone book, try to find that elusive number, and make my peace with the red-tape idiots.

I'd rather go to jail.

Actually, jail might not be all that bad. I have a friend in New York, an old college chum, who has seven children. She received a traffic ticket a couple of years ago for negligent driving. It seems she innocently turned the wrong way on a one-way freeway, and some cad refused to get out of her way. Unfortunately, the cad proved to be an off-duty highway patrolman, so my pal Jill had to appear in court.

Much to everyone's surprise (except mine), when the judge said, "Fifteen dollars and costs or two days in jail," Jill quickly replied in happy anticipation:

"Oh, I'll take the two days in jail!"

She didn't get it. Unfortunately for Jill, her husband heard about it, paid the fine, and had her back in the kitchen by noon. Too bad. Jill really needed those two days in jail.

You think I'm crazy? Just look at it from a mother's point of view. Two whole days, forty-eight lovely hours, in a nice, quiet jail cell. Six meals, each of which is planned by somebody else, cooked by somebody else, and served by somebody else, probably brought to me on a tray in my room. (I would, of course, demand solitary confinement; that's the least they could do.) After the repast, a "servant" would swoop away my tray, and that wonderful somebody else would wash the dishes.

I could read all evening, without interruption. I could get to bed early, and stay there all night! Everybody would get their own drinks of water, and find their own way to the bathroom. Nobody would ask me to get up to check the thermostat, or to let the dog out, or to let the teenagers in.

Come morning, I could sleep as late as I wanted. Noisy? Who cares? It's never too noisy for a mother to sleep; in fact, there is nothing more soothing than the sounds of somebody else scrubbing a floor or running a vacuum cleaner.

If two guards began to fight over whose turn it was to carry trays or wash the dishes, I wouldn't have to do a thing about it. They could kill each other for all I care. And if their noisy bickering disturbed the warden's nap, it wouldn't be my problem. Let him handle his own kids . . . ooops, I mean guards. I wouldn't even have to worry if they got into the warden's desk and took his car keys!

Ah, jail. It may not be a weekend in Las Vegas, but who wants to go to Las Vegas? They have telephones in Vegas. In jail, the kids couldn't call me.

Maybe I won't file that tax form, after all.

15

Has anybody seen my shoes?

When I was a young girl (Yes, children, I was once a young girl), a popular campus-question was, "If you were stranded on a desert island, what one book would you choose to take with you, and what one person would you want to be stranded with?"

My answer depended on the decade in which the question was asked. In the 1930s I wouldn't have hesitated at all to choose the *Wizard of Oz* and my father. In the 1940s, the book would have been *Gone With the Wind*, but who's going to spend time reading when you are all alone on a desert island with Frank Sinatra? The 1950s? A cookbook and my bridegroom.

Since then, however, the question is not so easy to answer. As for the book, almost anything will do as I love to read, but how does a lady choose between the man she wants and the man she needs? I'd want to take my husband, but I'd have to take St. Anthony, because even on a deserted island with my total possession being one single book, I'd lose the darn thing and need St. Anthony to help me find it.

I am a born loser. I lose everything: my car keys, my glasses, my purse, my pens, my mind. I have even been known to lose one or two of the kids on occasion, which is easily understandable to anyone who has ever gone anyplace with eight or nine kids all at the same time.

Just the other day I took Peggy, Annie, Timmy, and Pat to the Westroads to buy school shoes, and in the crowded mall, I lost Timmy. We finally found him, and as we made our way through the parking lot, I realized I couldn't remember where I had left the car. Fortunately, Peggy remembered, but it didn't do us much good; once we got to the car I discovered I had lost my keys.

So we hailed a taxi, went all the way home, got the second set of keys, went back to the parking lot, and as I opened my purse to pay the taxi driver I realized I had lost my billfold.

This was just one of the times I lost my mind.

Every morning for the past twenty years I have had to call upon St. Anthony to help me find gym shoes, school sweaters, homework assignments, history books, Danny's glasses, and, on more than one occasion, Danny. That boy is so absentminded he can't remember where he is supposed to be, when, and why.

While the presence of St. Anthony is an absolute necessity on school mornings, most of our searches are seasonal.

In the summer, St. Anthony and I dig through dresser drawers looking for swimsuits which my kids swear they carefully stored away last Labor Day. We always find them . . . in the swim-club locker, mildewed and ruined, but that's not St. Anthony's fault. He just finds things; he doesn't work miracles.

In the autumn, St. Anthony and I search for lightweight jackets or sweaters for the kids to wear on those chilly fall days which aren't quite cold enough for winter coats, and when winter comes and the first snow flies, St. Anthony does seem to work a miracle when he not only finds the boots but makes them match.

It is in the spring that I really keep St. Anthony busy, for there is so much to search for in the spring: the basketball, the bikes, the tennis rackets and roller skates, the baseball bat and mitts, and the sweaters and lightweight jackets we found last fall and lost during the winter.

Where *do* all the jackets go? This year we looked in all the obvious places: under the beds, in the back of the car, on the shelf in the garage, behind the refrigerator, and even at the bottom of the ironing basket. (Anybody lose a bunting?)

An intensive inquiry uncovered the following facts: Danny left his in the sacristy and an absentminded acolyte evidently wore it home. (If there are acolytes more absentminded than Danny, the Church really is in trouble.)

Jim reluctantly admitted that he had tossed his into the air in a triumphant cheer at the last football game and, like the proverbial arrow, "it fell to earth, he knew not where."

Mary thinks hers is in her locker at school, but she's not sure, since she lost the key last October and hasn't been able to get in there since.

Peggy left her jacket at Kathy Somebody's house, but the Somebodys moved to California at Christmastime, presumably with Peggy's jacket.

Tim and Patrick uncovered two jackets which I did not purchase and have never seen before but which undoubtedly belong to Matthew and Jacob Frievald, our backyard neighbors. Since Sue Frievald has nine sons, and I have seven, we long ago gave up trying to identify boys' clothing "left at our house." It's enough trouble identifying the boys.

Annie's jacket is "at school someplace; probably in lost and found" where I will, in desperation, send all the rest of the kids to find coats, any coats, for parochial schools have an unwritten law: "If it's been here more than a month and it fits, it's yours."

Even more difficult to find than the jackets is the spring sports equipment.

"Who took my basketball?" Tim will ask. "I left it right here on the sofa last November." I can't imagine why it isn't still there. I would stake my life on the fact that not one of my children, on finding a grubby basketball on the living-room sofa, would say to himself: "Oh, here is a basketball on the sofa. I shall put it away where it belongs."

The basketball is found outdoors under the bushes where it withered through the winter because some angry mother threw it there.

For some ridiculous reason, the baseball mitts are not on the bathroom counter. On top of the refrigerator perhaps? Of course!

When we opened the broom closet to look for the roller skates, we found the tennis rackets, but no skates.

Ignoring my husband's comment: "You mean they're not on the steps? I thought you always kept your roller skates on the steps!" we finally found the skates in, of all places, the toy box.

"Well, who would have thought to look there?" asked Annie, logically.

Incredibly, the bikes were exactly where they were supposed to be: turned upside down in the basement, waiting for their owners to check gears and repair brakes, but as yet nobody has because: "Gee, Mom, we couldn't get to the tool bench with the bikes in the way." If they knew they couldn't reach the tools because the bikes were there, how come they claimed they didn't know the bikes were there?

When St. Anthony isn't searching for winter coats or roller skates in the storage closets and broom cabinets, he is rumbling through my "Thing" drawer, helping my husband find his pliers.

Every housewife has a Thing drawer, so-called because that's where she keeps Things: scissors, tools, pencils, Band-Aids, warranties for appliances that broke down long ago and were thrown away, a deck of cards which will be complete as soon as we find the jack of clubs, holy cards which have remained homeless since Catholics quit carrying missals; raffle tickets,

Easter seals, and shoelaces which are guaranteed to disappear when needed. In fact, everything in the Thing drawer carries that guarantee, due to the fact that all Thing drawers have no back. They go on and on, into infinity, and anything left in there over twenty-four hours tends to drift back into the Great Nowhere. Consequently, even St. Anthony is often thwarted in his search for things in the Thing drawer.

Either that or he just refuses to cooperate with my husband, and if that's the case, I really can't blame him, because my husband certainly never wants to cooperate with him.

You see, my husband doesn't believe in saints. Oh, he believes in their existence; he just doesn't believe in bothering them. He thinks that if a guy has spent seventy or eighty years on earth getting sanctified and maybe even martyred, he shouldn't have to spend his eternity being pestered with petitions from sinners. Actually, my husband is just a typical executive; he doesn't believe in wasting time working with the underlings. If you want something done right, go to the Boss.

Now I have great faith in St. Anthony's Boss, but I do hate to bother Him with trivial matters, so when my husband borrowed and then misplaced Michael's calculator, I called the kids together and told them we would make the novena to St. Anthony.

"Can't it wait a week or two?" asked Peg. "This is such a great treat, I'd like to enjoy it awhile."

"What do you mean, a great treat?" I asked her.

"*Dad* lost something for a change," she grinned. "Usually we're the ones responsible and Dad blows his top and campuses us or fines us our allowances. But this time it's *his* fault. Can't we dig him just a little?"

"Don't bother," said Mike. "I just mentioned it to him, and he said it's *my* fault."

"How could it be your fault?" asked Mary. "I thought Dad used it last."

"He did," answered Mike, "but he said he wouldn't have lost it if I hadn't loaned it to him in the first place."

Monday night my husband said: "I thought I might have taken that calculator to the office, but it isn't there. You didn't find it here at home, did you?"

"No," I replied, "and we looked everywhere."

"Then it's gone," he said.

"It isn't gone," I told him. "Where could it go? Nobody took it out of this house, so it must be here someplace."

"Then why can't you find it?" he asked logically.

"You don't understand," I explained patiently. "I don't find things. I look for things. St. Anthony finds them. And when St. Anthony is ready to find that calculator, he will put it where I can see it. If you are in a hurry for it, I suggest *you* speak to St. Anthony."

He shrugged off my suggestion, but I knew he was concerned, and felt a little guilty, because he had lost Mike's calculator. Every day he came home from work and asked if we had found the calculator, and every day I resisted the urge to ask him if he had prayed to St. Anthony (while Mike resisted the urge to ask who was going to replace the calculator).

On Friday we found the calculator, caught in a loose bracket behind Mike's desk.

"Oh, golly," groaned Mike. "Dad must have returned it to me after all. He'll never let me hear the end of this. Can't we just sneak it into his bureau drawer and let him find it?"

"Nothing doing," I told him. "Dad would just be tempted to sneak it into your desk drawer, and the two of you could spend the rest of the year shifting blame. I'll call him and tell him we found it."

"Guess what?" I asked my husband when he answered the phone.

"You found the calculator," he replied confidently.

"How did you know?" I asked. "Say, did you finally say a prayer to St. Anthony?"

"No," he replied. "But I stopped at St. John's for noon Mass and spoke to God about it."

If my Beloved knows God *that* well, maybe I'll choose him for that desert island after all.

16

What's my line?

One of my pet peeves is the registration form which asks for "Occupation of Spouse." Since this particular spouse is unoccupied, I never know what to put down. My feminist friends freak out if I admit to being "just a housewife," so I try to enter into the spirit of the thing and claim a profession.

Last week I was faced with another "occupation of spouse" and I cheerfully put down "Plumber." It was not a lie; last week I *was* a plumber. Due to the fact that Patrick had tried to flush his toothbrush down the toilet, our dining room ceiling began to rain, and as it was after 5 P.M. (Naturally it was after 5 P.M.; Section 32 of the Plumber's Code stipulates that plumbing is to be installed in such a manner that it will never break down during working hours), I fixed it myself. It wasn't difficult. Any mother who has spent twenty years retrieving toy trucks from her toilet, and repairing the damage of dozens of teen shampoos to shower drains, qualifies for a plumber's license.

That was last week. This week, when I registered the girls for a drama course, I listed myself as "waiter." The teacher will undoubtedly assume that I am a waitress who doesn't know her masculine from her feminine, but the truth is, this week I have been, in the literal sense of the word, a waiter.

On Monday, Timmy injured his thumb playing baseball, so I took him to the pediatrician where we waited two hours for the doctor to wiggle Tim's thumb and announce: "This thumb is injured."

"I know the thumb is injured, Doctor," I said, "but is it broken?"

"That is not for me to say," he said. "It must be x-rayed." So I had to take Tim over to the hospital, where we waited another hour for the technician to x-ray the thumb, and another forty-five minutes for the radiologist to read the X ray and give the results to the technician, who in turn gave them to the pediatrician, who finally informed me that "The thumb is not broken."

Swell. How do you go home and tell your husband that you have just spent three hours and $35 on a thumb that doesn't even have the decency to be broken?

On Tuesday, I went to pick up Danny at his basketball game and had to wait twenty-five minutes while the game went into overtime. If football games can end in a tie, why are basketball games allowed to go on forever?

On Wednesday, I went to pick up Peggy at choir practice and had to wait twenty minutes while Sister Callista convinced the kids that "It's the Real Thing" might be great for Coca-Cola, but it won't do for the Communion hymn.

On Thursday, I went shopping and spent half an afternoon waiting to get waited on, and when I finally did get waited on, I had to wait while the clerk who was waiting on me went to answer the phone. Why is it that when I am a telephone-shopper, I must wait if the clerk has a customer, but if I am the customer, I wait while she answers the phone? I must *look* like a waiter.

On Friday, my husband and I went to a movie where we

waited to buy tickets, waited to buy popcorn, waited to get a seat, waited for the feature to start, and then waited (impatiently!) for it to be over. (I can't bring myself to walk out on a movie I paid $4.00 to see.)

On Saturday, I went to pick up the kids at the swimming pool and waited half an hour while one or the other of them ran back to look for towels, sunglasses, sun lotion, transistor radios, and each other. Never send one of your children to look for another; you may be a waiter forever.

This week I am also, however reluctantly, a bookie. I don't take the bets; I just hold the money. As everyone knows, we Catholics are devout gamblers. (And I am not here referring to Vatican Roulette . . . at that, we're not too devout.) We control the bingo business, as well as the card parties, but our big line is raffles. If a parishioner donates anything from a chocolate cake to a Cadillac, you can be sure the nuns and the priests will want to raffle it off.

This has been a record raffle week at our house, and my non-mathematical mind has never been so boggled. The parish issued chance books for its annual fund-raising raffle, while at the same time the Jesuits at Creighton Prep issued chance books for a raffle to be held at their annual BASH. (I know what you are thinking, but it really means Building A Scholastic Heritage.)

I don't mind buying the chances and contributing to these worthy events. I was born and raised a Catholic and spent sixteen years in Catholic schools where we learned an infallible doctrine: If you are going to raise Catholic kids, you better budget for the annual raffle. No, it's not the donating I object to; it's the bookkeeping.

Seven of our kids were selling chances this week, as some of them were in on the parish raffle, and others were working on BASH. At the same time, I had been issued two chance books from the parish Ladies Guild, and my husband had two books from BASH. This meant I had to keep track of $121 worth of raffle tickets. Each book for the parish raffle held eleven tickets, at $1.00 a ticket, but if the seller sold the whole book he could keep the eleventh dollar as commission.

Our kids, working for that eleventh dollar, enthusiastically went about the neighborhood selling raffle tickets. Since our neighborhood is predominantly Catholic, this meant that the neighbors' children came to sell to me. (In other words, we mothers just trade money.) This year I'm afraid I didn't do much trading since the prize for both raffles was a brand-new sports car, and I was afraid that I might win one or both of them. If there is anything I do not need, it's another car. It's not just the gasoline bills, taxes, and insurance that bother me, it's the fact that I already spend my weekend nights waiting up for one son to wreck the sedan and another son to wreck the station wagon, and I am not about to put a third and possibly fourth son into a sports car.

But as I said, it's not the money I mind, it's the accounting. Jim and Mary each sold one book and assured me that their money was safely tucked away. Peggy and Annie each turned in $8.00, and Tim outdid them by selling nine tickets. Danny turned in $7.50 and (not unusual for Danny) can't explain the fifty cents differential but promised to make it up out of his allowance. Poor little Patrick only sold one chance, but he seemed happy about it, so I didn't push him to sell more.

As I was responsible for the money as well as the stubs, I spent the entire weekend coordinating tickets and stubs and counting and recounting money. I had the right number of signed stubs, and the correct number of unsold tickets, but the money wouldn't balance. I kept coming up $1.00 short.

I called together the croupiers, and after a brief conference, the dollar was found. It seems that Patrick had withheld it.

"Patrick, why didn't you turn in your dollar?" I asked.

"Because it's mine," he said.

"How do you figure that?" I asked. "You only sold one ticket."

"Yeah," he explained, "I know. But I started at the back of the book and sold the eleventh ticket, and Sister says that's mine."

I wish Patrick had been selling the tickets for BASH; only a Jesuit can refute that logic.

17

Here comes Santa

I hate to admit this, but my husband is a heretic.

He believes in God, the doctrines of the Church, and the infallibility of the Fighting Irish, but he denies one universally accepted truth which, if not exactly dogma, certainly should be, and that is, the existence of Santa Claus.

Can you imagine a father of ten children not believing in Santa Claus? It's ridiculous; it's unrealistic; it's heretical.

I'll tell you, it's not easy, living with a Yuletide Heretic. He's not a Scrooge, you understand; he's just a guy who insists on facing facts, and as far as I'm concerned, nothing spoils Christmas faster than facing facts.

So when he looks under our tree every Christmas and asks: "Where did all those presents come from?" I always answer: "Santa Claus brought them!" Do you think I'm going to spoil my holiday season by reminding myself that come January first, Santa's going to send a bill?

Despite my heretical husband (and also because of him), our Christmas is always wild and wonderful. Actually, Christmas itself is fairly mild; it's Christmas Eve that is chaotic, for while most families spend the night before Christmas snuggling in their beds and dreaming of sugar plums, the Bloomingdales are wallowing in wrapping paper and ribbons, enjoying an early Noel.

For as long as I can remember, Santa has come to our house, not on Christmas morn, but on Christmas Eve. The reason for this goes back to the days of my childhood when my father, a newspaperman, had to work on Christmas Day. (In those days, newspapers published seven days a week, holidays included.) In order that we might enjoy Christmas with my father (who, unlike my husband, was not a heretic for the simple reason that my mother handled the household budget and she never let him know that Santa Claus cost money), we celebrated Santa on Christmas Eve.

This became a family tradition, which I later imposed upon my own husband with the rather convincing argument that soon we would have kids and did he really want to get up at 5 A.M. on Christmas morning and be jolly? Frankly, I wouldn't get up at five to greet a combined calling committee of the Pope, the President, and Robert Redford (well . . . maybe Redford); I certainly wouldn't get up to greet Santa. My husband acquiesced; if I insisted on Santa, we might as well let him come on Christmas Eve.

So, for the past twenty-three years, St. Nicholas has blessed the Bloomingdales on the night before Christmas, and in the days when we still had tiny children, the confusion and chaos were incredible.

Every Christmas Eve, after the dinner dishes were dried and put away, my husband would take the Believers for a ride, to see the Christmas lights and decorations, while the non-Believers would stay home to help me greet Santa. As soon as the carload of excited children would pull out of the drive, "Santa's helpers" and I would dash to the storage closet and spend a frantic hour putting a little red wagon together, or testing toy cars and trucks (and running to the store for batteries that worked), dressing up dolls, setting up games, discarding telltale boxes and packing, and rechecking lists to be sure that the little boys didn't get the dolls and the girls, boxing gloves.

By eight o'clock, with toys in place, tree glowing, and the heretic impatiently honking in the driveway, we would signal that Santa had come and gone.

It was at that moment that the Yuletide spirit descended, in the form of little children barreling through the door, tossing their coats in wild disarray, pausing only momentarily to take in the glorious display of toys and trying to decide "which pile is mine?" Always, always they knew. The toy piano was Peggy's of course, and the roller skates were for Ann; the toy cars and trucks, so similar in color and make, were quickly claimed by Tim and Pat, each knowing instinctively which was meant for whom. No toys were tagged; each child just *knew* what was his; there was never a tear; each one had been granted his wish. (Another miracle of Christmas: Mother's remarkable memory!)

Little voices squealed in delight as dolls were picked up and hugged; trucks were banged and crashed and whirred off in every direction; harmonicas and xylophones rang out in chaotic cacophony. It was loud, confusing, and wonderful.

What is more fun than watching little children enjoying Christmas? It's watching your big children watching your little children enjoying Christmas. Is that big lug with the silly grin on his face—and, by golly, is that a tear in his eye?—dwelling on a Christmas past, when another little red wagon was his? Or is he contemplating a Christmas hence, when he won't be at home to enjoy this glorious noise?

And so it would go, into the night and early morning. There would be songs and games and sneaking fruitcake and candy, and, finally, bedtime for the Believers, and Clean-up Time for the non-Believers.

Christmas morning was less chaotic. The excitement of the toys now gave way to the real reason for Christmas: the birthday of Jesus. For Christmas Mass, we often attended the midmorning Mass at a nearby monastery where, at the sight of us, the monks would smile silently and bow their heads, undoubtedly in humble gratitude that they "had chosen the better part."

The long day was filled with playing games and trading toys and interpreting rules and directions, stuffing the turkey and eating it, clearing away the dishes and cleaning up the kitchen, and realizing, with sweet sadness at the end of the evening when tired children were tucked into bed, that there is nothing so *over* as Christmas.

Our Christmases, when our children were tiny, were exhausting and expensive, but it was worth it. I loved it; I miss it; I know, I'm crazy.

Now that the children are all old enough to be non-Believers, we have Christmas "as it should be." All the gifts will be carefully wrapped and tagged and put under the tree; they will be opened on Christmas Eve, but there will be no ride, no suspense, no Santa. I don't think I'm going to like it very much.

I was bemoaning this fact to my mother, who listened silently, then patted my hand and said:

"Cheer up, Teresa. Santa Claus hasn't deserted you; he is just on sabbatical. He'll be back one Christmas, when you have a houseful of grandchildren, and then Christmas will be better than ever, for there will be the same toys, the same joys, the same noise . . . with an added holiday bonus: when the baby gets cranky, everybody goes home!"

"Now!" she said firmly, turning to her married grandchildren, "you heard your mother; she wants Santa Claus here . . . by Christmas!"

Are you listening, children?

Part V

It takes a heap o' livin' in a house t' make it home . . .
EDGAR GUEST, Home

18

The terrible tornado of 1975

It all started with the basketball stand. A March wind blew it down, and as every mother of teenage boys knows, you can get along without a house, but you can't survive without a basketball stand.

When we went to replace the basketball stand, we concluded that this time we would set it in a concrete base.

This meant getting a cement mixer to come out to the house, and we decided as long as we had to go to that expense, we might as well patch the back steps at the same time.

But the driver of the cement mixer convinced us that it would be a waste of time and money to patch concrete steps; our extremes in Nebraska weather would just cause them to crumble again, and anyway, a house as large and lovely as ours should not be spoiled by mended steps. So we agreed to let him tear them out and put in new ones.

While the men were working on the new steps, the little kids were hanging on the back storm door, swinging back and forth,

watching the workmen. In due course the storm door sprung, so
we had to buy a new one.

The new door looked beautiful beside the new steps; what did
not look beautiful was the old back porch. So we painted it.
This made the rest of the house look rather crummy, so we decided to paint it, too. However, since the house was so huge and
so high, we decided we must hire professional painters to complete the job. But the professional painters refused to paint the
house until we had hired a carpenter to fix the wood trim and a
sheet-metal worker to repair the gutters, which we did. Since the
painters had to remove the combination storm windows, we decided this would be a good time to get the glaziers out to repair
the two windows which somebody shot a beebee through when
he was trying to hit the pigeons roosting on our chimney.

Once they all got finished, the house was gorgeous . . . on
the outside. The inside, by comparison, was awful, so, since the
painters were still around, we had them redo the downstairs and
a couple of bedrooms upstairs.

Now I suppose you have concluded that I then went out and
bought all new furniture. You're wrong. I was going to, but the
week after the painters finished, a tornado hit our property. It
took everything but the basketball stand.

How does one write about a tornado which destroys her home
and everything in it? One is inclined to curse and to cry, but
what's the point in that? It's easier to look for some humor
(however hysterical!), some reason, some resignation, and a will
to rebuild or replace, refurnish or restore the necessities, and to
forget about the little luxuries which are lost forever.

The triple tornado which destroyed our home hit Omaha, Nebraska, at 4:45 P.M. on Tuesday, May 6, 1975. It had been a
beautiful spring morning, but by afternoon our spacious skies
had darkened and a hint of rain was in the air. Nine of our ten
children had obediently come straight home from school when
teachers told them to "hurry home now; the sky looks strange."

Our eldest son, Lee III, was at work, where he had a part-time job in his dad's office.

At 4 P.M. Dan, Peggy, Ann, Tim, and Patrick had persuaded me to let them turn on the usually forbidden-on-a-school-day television to watch "The Mouseketeers," which had just made a long-awaited comeback. Our teenagers, John, Mike, Jim, and Mary, were in their rooms studying for final exams.

I was in the kitchen, making hamburger patties for an early dinner, when the kids called from the TV room:

"Hey, Mom, there's a tornado watch on."

I wasn't too concerned. We Omahans don't panic at tornado watches; they are as frequent as spring showers. But for some reason, I felt this one might be different; the sky *was* strange, the gray clouds had a greenish-hue, so when our fifteen-year-old Jim asked if he could go to the store, just a couple of blocks away, I suggested he wait awhile "just to see what the weather does."

What the weather did was unbelievable, and horrible. At 4:29 the civil defense sirens began to blare, indicating that the tornado "watch" had been changed to a tornado "warning." A funnel had been sighted. Even then we didn't seek shelter (we would today; on that day we learned a profound respect for that siren), but four minutes later, at 4:33, another bulletin reported that a funnel had touched down in southwest Omaha, causing undetermined damage. It was then that I ordered the children to the basement. The little ones scampered downstairs immediately; the teenagers, however, insisted on standing at the southwest dining-room window, watching the sky grow even blacker as the wind began to whip the trees.

A few seconds later they saw the funnel, a massive cornucopia of dark debris, whirling directly toward our three-story, nineteen-room home. For one awful moment they were paralyzed, and terrified, as they hypnotically watched that funnel snatch up houses and cars, and hundreds of appliances from the huge Sidles warehouse on Seventy-fourth and Pacific, southwest of our home. Finally, Mike and Jim tore themselves from the terrible sight and dashed to the basement, tripping over each other in an effort to reach shelter.

"What's it doing out there?" I asked Mike. I wasn't frightened; I had never been in a tornado before; I had never even been close to one. I thought if we were hit, we might lose a few shingles off the roof or even a couple of windows. "What did you see?"

"One helluva funnel," said Mike, "and it's headed right this way."

And indeed it was. When it was still a mile away we could feel the pressure on our skin, as if we were being squashed by some invisible force. The noise was incredible. I had heard that the noise of a tornado is comparable to a loud freight train; this is true only in that it goes CLACK-CLACK-CLACK. I have never heard such a terrible sound, but I imagine it is like the wail of banshees screaming in cacophony with the demons in hell. It came like a thousand jets at rooftop level, the roar accompanied by banging and battering, twisting and tearing.

The triple funnel first tore through Bergan Mercy Hospital, where nuns and nurses had quickly moved patients to shelter, and where Dr. Joseph McCaslin, treating a heart patient in the emergency ward, courageously continued with emergency cardiac care which saved his patient's life.

The funnel then sliced through Sidles, removed the top floor of the newly built, luxurious 7400 Plaza Building, and then turned east to Seventy-second Street (Omaha's famous Strip), only to veer north again to terrorize but not injure nine thousand spectators at the Ak-sar-ben race track. It whirled back and forth across Seventy-second Street, leveling the mammoth, multi-million-dollar Nebraska Furniture Mart and ripping apart the solid brick Farmer's Union Insurance Building.

Then, as if seeking another juicy victim, it spotted our big white house on a Seventieth Avenue hill, and it struck.

The electricity exploded, leaving our basement shelter in total darkness, and then I did panic. I had forgotten to turn anything off; we had a gas furnace, gas stove, and gas hot-water heater. I waited for another explosion. (It did not come.) As I fought hysteria, I suddenly became aware of the incredible calmness of my children.

Sixteen-year-old Mike, fifteen-year-old Jim, and fourteen-year-old Mary had each reached for a younger sibling and held tightly to eight-year-old Annie, seven-year-old Tim, and our youngest, Patrick, who was only five. Danny, eleven, and ten-year-old Peggy had always been close siblings, but never so close as they were at that moment, clinging to each other. Our toy poodle, Mimi, shivered at my feet, as terrified as the rest of us. I gave a brief thought to Dolly, our aging Irish setter, who had been sleeping on the front porch. Where was she now? Under the porch, scared but safe; she survived.

The banshees wailed even louder as the demons rolled back our huge Spanish-tile roof and sucked our entire third floor into the venomous mouth. Every door was slammed, again and again; every one of our sixty-seven windows was shattered and then sucked into the funnel, leaving a blanket of glass shards across the plowed-up lawns.

Furniture was hurled from room to room, from block to block, and replaced by heavy filing cabinets and computers from a neighboring bank.

We didn't know all this immediately, of course. All we knew was noise, and that terrible pressure inside our heads and outside our bodies.

How long did it last? A few seconds? Minutes? Forever? I honestly don't know. *Too* long, that I do know. It was over suddenly, shockingly; and the silence was all around us, eerie and weird and as frightening as the noise that had preceded it.

I couldn't bring myself to go upstairs. I made our seventeen-year-old son, John, who had brazened out the storm in his basement bedroom, go first, and we cautiously followed. As he forced open the door leading into the kitchen, he paused a moment, then said, softly:

"Oh my God."

The kitchen was a shambles; our huge double-oven stove now stood in the center of the room; cabinet doors were blown off; yet . . . incredibly . . . my crystal goblets stood untouched in those same cabinets.

In the dining room our ten-foot refectory table had been crushed under the weight of a giant oak tree, which had sailed through the wall, leaving a gaping hole. Furniture was disarranged as if a devil had moved it by magic spell, smashing it against the walls, even moving some of it into the next room.

In our lovely thirty-five-foot living room, every piece of furniture was ruined. A heavy typewriter which had been resting on a card table in the corner was gone; we never did find it. A strange bicycle stood in the center of the room; we had no idea to whom it belonged. A soiled apron, not mine . . . a neighbor's, I presume . . . hung from a picture hook where a portrait of the Sacred Heart had formerly graced our home.

I looked out the windows that were no longer there and tried to cry, but I couldn't. For blocks around us homes had been leveled, trees uprooted, shrubs stripped bare. I thought of the family behind us, with seven little children. Were they all dead? Was everybody dead?

Nothing moved. No one appeared. The silence was terrifying. Later we realized the strange silence was due to the death of nature: there were no leaves left to rustle; no insects to hum; no birds to sing. I have never heard before or since, the terrible "sounds of silence" we heard that day.

The silence was suddenly broken by a crash of thunder, followed by cold, heavy rain bringing with it hail and more wind. With no windows and no roof, the muddy water ruined the few things that might have been saved.

Having finished the destruction, the rain quickly followed the tornado which had preceded it; the skies cleared, and a bright May sun shone on our shattered world.

Slowly, cautiously, as if they were afraid of what they would find, the neighbors began to appear on what remained of their porches and patios. For one moment we simply stared at each other, then they called:

"Are you all right? Is everybody all right?"

"Yes. Are you?" Yes. Miraculously, we were all right. Only three people were killed in the tornado which had continued north up Seventy-second Street, demolishing part of Creighton Prep, our Jesuit high school; destroying Lewis and Clark Junior High, a synagogue, the Omaha Community Playhouse, churches, stores, homes, and office buildings. In all, it devastated a total of nine hundred square blocks and left three hundred persons injured, though none of them were in our block.

Within minutes the streets filled with people, some coming to help, others to gawk and even to loot.

As I made my way across our living room, a young man dashed through the front door, stared at us, and suddenly began to cry. His tears were quickly replaced by an embarrassed grin, as he said:

"I saw . . . I saw your house blow away. I was watching . . . from our house (four blocks away) . . . and I saw your third floor just *go*. I thought you were dead," said Mike Rouse, a senior at Prep and a classmate of our son John. Almost immediately, from the other direction, Mike's married brother, Jim, came running toward the house, carrying a desperately needed flashlight, for while dusk had not yet fallen, our basement, where gas and water had to be shut off, was pitch black.

As I headed back through the house toward the basement, a red-bearded giant climbed through a window shouting: "Anybody here injured?"

"No," I answered. "We are all right." This complete stranger then threw his arms around me and hugged me, as if to thank me for not being dead. Then, as quickly as he had come, he departed, through the same window, to continue his search for someone in need of help . . . or a hug.

Others were not so concerned; they had come to sight-see and to scavenge. They stared, pointed, took pictures, kicked through our rubble, picking up and carting away anything that took their fancy, while totally ignoring our cries of outrage and frustration. It was as if I were invisible; they stared at me and through me, wanting to share my excitement but not my sorrow.

My shock and anger turned to fury as I watched these idiots carelessly light cigarettes around overturned cars and broken gas mains. Who knew what explosive fumes might be in the air? But God blessed us: there were no explosions, no fires. Just sightseers and scavengers, crowding the streets to the point where it became impossible for husbands and fathers to reach their destroyed homes.

Husband and father! Panic really hit me as I thought of my husband and son. Where were they? How far had the tornado gone and in what direction? Had it hit my husband's office? Were they safe? Why didn't they come home?

I learned later that my husband was at his office, desperately trying to call home. But the lines were down; he could not get through. He finally contacted a neighbor, half a mile away, and asked her if the tornado had hit our area. She couldn't bring herself to tell him that she had seen our house demolished. She said simply: "You'd better go home."

It took my husband and son almost two hours to travel two miles; it was not so much the debris that blocked the streets, as it was the people. They finally left their car and walked the last quarter mile home.

Meanwhile, I was terrified, not knowing where they were and also fearing my husband's reaction to the dreadful sight. Consequently, I made all nine children stand in the middle of the street so, when he turned the corner, my husband would see that we were safe.

Finally I saw him, and I watched his face contort in fear and horror as he saw the beautiful home he had provided for us, now a blackened mass of crumbling stucco and broken glass. His steps quickened, and I realized he hadn't seen us; he didn't know where we were, or even *if* we were.

I ran to him, tripping over fallen electrical cords and felled trees, pushing my way through strolling sightseers and stunned neighbors. I threw myself into his arms and finally, at last, I cried.

"We are all right," I sobbed, repeating that beautiful phrase over and over. "All the children are here; we're all right. But our house . . . is gone. Oh, honey, I'm sorry! Our beautiful home is gone!"

He held me tight and smiled. "Sorry? Honey, it's not your fault!" (A family joke: everything that goes wrong is Mom's fault.) "Come on now," he said, "let's get the kids together and go home."

"Home?" I asked.

"Yes," he said calmly, and forced a laugh. "Home. I'm not too sure where home will be, but I promise you, I'll take you home."

And he did. It's a different house, of course, without a familiar piece of furniture in it. But with the same family, all safe and all together, it's home.

It took weeks before we saw any humor in that tornado, but, it being *my* tornado, I knew there had to be some. And there was.

The first laughter came when a reporter interviewed me and asked:

"What was your first thought, your first reaction, when you came up out of your basement and saw the damage and destruction?"

It was such a typical newspaper-reporter question, we had to laugh. But being from a newspaper family, I appreciated the reason for his question, and tried desperately to remember my reaction and to give him a newsworthy answer.

Before I could come up with a headliner, Timmy broke in
and said:

"I remember, Mama. You looked around the living room a
minute and then you said: 'Somebody get a broom; we've got to
get this mess cleaned up before your father gets home.'" I don't
believe that, but the kids swear it's true.

We all laughed again, a few days later, when the insurance
inspectors were assessing damage to the house. When they got to
the basement, they opened the door of John's bedroom and exclaimed:

"My God! It really went through here. What a mess!"

That was the only room in the house that the tornado hadn't
touched.

We took pictures of our demolished home and sent them to
my mother who looked at them silently and then commented
softly:

"God works in wondrous ways. At last Teresa has figured out
how to avoid spring housecleaning."

Spring housecleaning that year was replaced by spring house
hunting, and God's wondrous works continued, for within five
weeks He had led us to a beautiful new home, which was vacant
and ready for occupancy. We occupied.

If you must move, that is the ideal way to do it. No packing
boxes, no moving vans, no trunks full of clothes. Nothing. Just
Mother and Dad and the kids and, of course, the insurance
check. Terrific.

19

Making the move

What was not so terrific was the five weeks of house hunting. Our immediate problem was not, however, where we would live eventually, but where would we live now? What does a family of twelve do when night is falling and their home is uninhabitable?

We did the only thing plausible: we checked into a hotel. The management was wonderful, welcoming us with open arms and discounted rates, until evening, when Timmy and Pat commandeered the elevators to play rocket ship, and the rocket broke down between planets.

The next morning God worked another wonder in the form of a phone call from an old friend who insisted that we take their lakeside cabin just a few miles west of Omaha.

"How perfect!" I told my husband. "I would never inflict these children on someone's home, but a cabin is ideal. If there aren't enough cots, we can rent sleeping bags. I'm sure there will be a little cooking stove, and we can borrow a cooler to use for an icebox. I won't have to worry about the kids causing any damage; who can hurt an old cabin?"

We quickly checked out of the hotel, piled into the second-hand station wagon my husband had hurriedly bought that morning, and headed for our temporary home. As we drove out west Dodge highway, toward the lake area, I began to be apprehensive, but I certainly wasn't prepared for what we found. The cabin was not quite like the little log cabins I had known as a child visiting the lake of the Ozarks. It was, in fact, a stone cottage, and when I opened the door I looked inside, gasped, and held out my arms like a patrol boy stopping school kids.

"Hold it!" I ordered. "Nobody goes in there!"

"What's the matter?" asked my husband. "Is the place a mess? Don't worry, we'll clean it up. You've got to expect a summer cabin to be a little musty and dusty."

"A little must and dust I'd welcome," I told him. "Take a look."

He stuck his head in the door, sighed, and said: "I see what you mean. We can't let our kids stay here."

But we had no choice; where else could we go? So, cautioning the kids to *please* be careful, I led them into the "cabin" which, to put it mildly, was *not* a mess. Nor was it a cabin, or even a cottage. It was a gorgeous summer home, lacking only a photographer to put it in the pages of *House Beautiful* or *Town and Country*. (He may have been there earlier; I wouldn't doubt it.)

There was ankle-deep wall-to-wall carpeting, a two-story cathedral-ceilinged living room with a natural-rock wall built around a massive wood-burning fireplace. The entire south wall was one huge picture window, overlooking a lovely lake and draped with electronically controlled, ceiling-to-floor hangings.

On the opposite wall was a balcony, off of which were four large bedrooms and a luxurious bath. The master bedroom, with its own bath and dressing room, opened off a corridor leading from the living room, which housed amid tables, lamps, and chairs, a three-tiered electric organ, a fully stocked wet bar, a stereo system, and an eight-foot genuine-leather sofa.

On the lower level, a rec room sported a professional pool table, another wet bar, a soda fountain, elaborate fishing equipment, and glory be! a washer and dryer.

I hesitantly opened the garage door and found, not the expected automobile, but an exquisite, late-model motor launch.

"Are you sure Jim and Marge know we have ten kids?" I asked my husband.

"Of course they do," he said as he led me back up to the all-electric kitchen. "Why else would Marge have this ten-pound roast cooking in the oven? And look, she stocked the pantry with snacks and pop, and the freezer with popsicles and ice cream."

I sat down and cried, weeping not so much in gratitude for having such wonderful friends as in fear of how I would explain to those friends that somebody poked a hole in their leather sofa, or spilled Kool-Aid on their carpet, or ripped the felt on their pool table, or . . .

"The kids will be good," said my husband. "Don't they always come through in a crisis?"

They do, and they did. They were terrific, taking care of their rooms, accepting responsibility for chores, helping with the cooking and cleaning . . . when they weren't falling into the lake.

That was our only problem. The proximity and attraction of the water. When my mother heard that I was afraid to leave the lake area to go into the city to house-hunt, she sent for the five younger children, intending to house all of them in her home. But my sisters and brother insisted on sharing the burden. That is true love, to take into your home and your heart a passel of nieces and nephews (not to mention two dogs), to feed them and clothe them, to calm their fears and wipe their tears, and assure them over and over that they will soon "go home." I will be forever grateful to Mother, Mary Helen, Art, Madeleine, Betsy, and Janet for their hospitality.

While the little kids were living it up at Grandma's, and the big kids were lying around the lakeshore, fishing, swimming and feeding the mosquitoes, I spent ten hours a day house hunting.

I hate house hunting. It's bad enough when you really want a new home; it's awful when you compare everything you see with the home you loved and lost. I imagine it is somewhat like choosing a second spouse, after having been married for years to "the Greatest." The follow-up had better be darn good.

In looking for a place to live, I wasn't worried about the reactions of the little kids. Home to them is wherever Mom and Dad are. But teenagers are something else again, for while they may decorate their own bedrooms in Contemporary Trash, they expect their home to look like Traditional Luxury. My husband, too, would be hard to please. If he had had his way we would still be living in our honeymoon apartment, with all ten kids stacked in the second bedroom. Men do not like to move, ever, for any reason. They don't begrudge the money, or the work involved; they just hate to reprogram their minds to drive home in a different direction.

So I reluctantly started house hunting and learned, in the process, a few hints which I will pass on to all of you who may be house hunting because your home got blown away by a tornado. (I can think of no other reason to move.)

When looking for a new home, go alone. Do not, under any circumstances, let your husband go with you. The first thing he will ask is the price, and if it's too high, you will be afraid to go through the house for fear you will fall in love with it and he won't let you buy it, and if it's too low, he will want to buy it even if you hate it.

Don't take your teenagers with you, for they will each insist on a private room with bath, and so what if the kitchen has a pump in the sink and a kerosene stove, look at the neat rec room! Also, if your teenagers are tagging along, you may find it difficult to keep from remarking:

"This house would be perfect if it just had one more bedroom. Say, honey, when do you think you will be leaving home?"

Don't take the little children with you, for no matter how many times you caution: "Don't touch!" they will, and you may end up buying the present owner's furniture if not his house.

So go house hunting alone, with only the necessary realtor who, if she has any sense at all, will keep her mouth shut and speak only when spoken to. Realtors should understand that a lady buyer doesn't want the facts about a house; she wants the feel of it. Let her walk through it slowly and silently, and in twenty minutes she can tell if it is right or wrong for her family. In the right house, she will feel "at home." She will be able to picture her family in the various rooms, at work, at play, awake or asleep. She can mentally place the Ping-Pong table, the baby's crib, and the gosh-awful painting from rich uncle Charlie. She will *want* the house. *Then* she may ask about the price and the taxes, the furnace and the foundation, but it won't make any difference. If she wants that house, she won't care if the roof leaks or the furnace fumes, here is home.

On the ninth of June, less than five weeks after the tornado turned us into nomads, we were settled in our new home, a gorgeous split-level with enough bedrooms, almost enough baths (are there ever enough?), a yard big enough for football, a patio perfect for picnics, and a kitchen even I can keep clean. My husband loves it; the children love it; I love it. But what's more important, the cleaning lady loves it. Who could ask for more?

Part VI

Hear me for my cause . . .

SHAKESPEARE, *Julius Caesar*

20

". . . Sincerely,"

To the Consolidated Tape and Record Club:

In reply to your letter of November 25 answering my letter of October 15 responding to your note of September 7 asking why I haven't replied to your August 1 request for payment of stereo tapes ordered July 1, let me state once again: they weren't. Ordered, that is. I did not order any tapes; I do not want any tapes; I will not pay for any tapes; I will not pay postage to return any tapes. True, I have received tapes, which are currently resting on my closet shelf. You may call for them at your convenience. A small storage charge is enclosed; prompt payment will avoid any finance charges.

Sincerely,

To the Sophisticated Book Club:

I am returning the book you offered for your November selection. By page twelve I had read in detail about abortion, adultery, arson, drug addiction, rape, incest, extortion, murder, and suicide. If God turned Lot's wife to a pillar of salt for simply catching a quick glimpse of Gomorrah, I tremble to think what He might do to me if I finish reading this book.

Sincerely,

Dear Mrs. Bombeck (or may I call you Erma?)

I don't suppose you subscribe to the Arbor Heights Junior High Parents Newsletter, but in case you happened to see their October issue, you might have read where I was referred to as the "local Erma Bombeck."

I am embarrassed about this, Erma, and if it will make you feel any better, you have my permission to refer to yourself as the "national Teresa Bloomingdale."

Fondly,

To the Manager, Brandeis Department Store:

As the Christmas season approaches, I have a request to make of you. Would you do me a favor? When my husband shows up to do his shopping in Pots and Pans, would you please direct him to Furs and Jewels? Thank you so much.

Gratefully,

To the Public Library:

I am sorry, but I cannot find the overdue copy of *Football Fanatics*. I have looked every place in the house except under Danny's bed, and if you think I am going to stick my hand under there, you're out of your mind. I know the policy is to pay for lost library books, but would you consider taking in trade two dozen copies of *I should have seen it coming when the rabbit died?*

Hopefully,

To the President of the Neighborhood Bank:

Would you please explain to me why the $100 I deposited on June 1 was not credited to my account until June 4, while the check I wrote at 10 A.M. June 3 bounced at noon on June 3? And why my husband was notified of the overdraft by 12:30?

You can cover the overdraft with the enclosed check, but please don't cash it before July 1 (or 5, depending on your crazy computer).

Sincerely,

Dear Father Pastor:

We have punished Patrick and Tim for sneaking into the back of church during the Ladies Altar Society Prayer Service and goofing off. However, I do think the ladies were a little strong in their accusation that it is a sacrilege to put goldfish in the holy water fonts. I thought we abolished sacrileges.

Incidentally, in these days of liberal liturgies, I am happy to know that we still have holy water in our holy water fonts. (But not nearly as happy as the goldfish.)

Pax vobiscum!

Dear Rise and Shine Clock Company:

I am returning your Wake-the-Dead alarm clock. It may work for a corpse, but it does nothing for a teenage boy. Would you have anything in stock with an alarm which rings with the magnetic tones of a teenline telephone?

Desperately,

Dear Mrs. Neighbor:

As school is due to start on Monday, would it be all right if I send your son home now? It's been fun having him for breakfast, lunch, and supper every day this summer, but I thought you might want to measure him for school clothes; he's grown so much since you sent him down to our house to play.

Incidentally, if What's-Her-Name is still at your house, will you tell her to stop by home on the way to school? We like to catch a glimpse of her every semester or so.

See you at PTA!

Sincerely,

Dear PTA Car-pool Chairman:

Please remove my name from the Car-pool Committee. My children have spent the summer taking walking lessons, and hopefully, they will all have their walking licenses by the time school starts.

Optimistically,

Dear Sister Principal:

Regarding the three-day suspension recently imposed on my son as punishment for whistling at the new novice (I warned you nuns about giving up your habits!), I would like to call to your attention the following facts:

1. Every morning of the suspension my son slept till noon.

2. Every afternoon of the suspension he played basketball, watched television, and bugged his mother.

3. Every evening of the suspension he reminded his brothers and sisters that "Ha, ha, ha, I don't have to go to school tomorrow!"

In the future, if any of my children misbehaves you have my permission to keep them after school, to make them scrub the classroom floors, to hang them by their thumbs. But if you send one more kid home for a three-day vacation I will picket the Pope for a twelve-month parochial-school year.

Peace!

To Congressman John Cavanaugh
House of Representatives
Washington, D.C.

Dear Congressman Cavanaugh:

As one of your constituents, I was surprised to note that you disapproved of a congressional pay raise on the grounds that you don't need the extra money and you don't know what you will do with it. This is to let you know what you will do with it.

In September, dear Congressman, your oldest child will start to school, and you will need most of that extra money to pay for his shoestrings, for the first lesson taught every kindergartner is: "Let's pull out our shoestrings and throw them away!" (The second lesson is: "Let's take off our shoes and hide them!" but I don't like to drop everything on you all at once.)

"For heaven's sakes!"—I can hear you saying—"I can afford shoestrings!"

That may be. It may even be that on a congressional salary

you can support a kindergartner. But what about next year? Do you really think that, as a one-income lawyer, you can afford to keep a first-grader in crayons?

Surely you remember the Crayon Rule from your own first-grade days. First-graders take a secret pledge among themselves to loan, lose, or snap in two, each and every crayon they own before the second week in September and any new ones before the third Tuesday of each month thereafter. With four little children so close in age, Congressman, you are going to invest so much money in crayons your critics may accuse you of subsidizing the Crayola Company.

Then there will be a subscription to *Weekly Reader*, membership in the Easy Reader Book Club, milk money, field-trip money, mission-box money, money for clever Halloween costumes so that your kids can be more ghoulish goblins than the other congressional kids, library fines (followed a week later by the purchase price of the fined but unfound book), numerous nickels to replace husky pencils (the kind daddies filch from the office won't do), and an indeterminate amount of money to buy a new bust of George Washington which one of the kids knocked off the pedestal but nobody will squeal, so your son will get socked for his share.

And that's just first grade. You will have many more years of raffle tickets, Christmas seals, scout cookies, band instruments, yearbooks, and "activity tickets" . . . the bane of every parent's pocketbook. And remember, Congressman, you have three more kids coming up.

So take your pay raise and run, John. And while you're running, run for President, because before you know it, your kids will be teenage drivers, and $200,000 a year will just about pay for automobile expenses.

Best of luck, John; God knows any man who finds himself both a father and a Congressman is going to need it.

Sincerely,

My darling Captain,

It pains me to tell you this, luv, but I can't see you anymore; our affair is over. It's not that I have stopped loving you; you are every bit as attractive as you were twenty years ago, when I first saw you in that dashing Navy uniform.

I remember how thrilled I was, the very morning after we met, when, after my husband went off to work, you paid me the first of so many memorable visits. I loved every hour spent with you, and wept on those days when you sent word that you couldn't come. Did you never realize that no one else could take your place?

I loved so much about you: your soft, gentle voice, never uttering a harsh or unkind word; your love of music and literature; your friends. Ah, those crazy friends of yours; I loved them almost as much as I love you.

How I shall miss you all! But what must be, must be, dear heart. We must end our long and happy relationship.

For you see, my love, our baby started to school this morning; we have no more babies at home, and I think it would look rather silly for a middle-aged mother to watch kiddie TV all by herself, don't you?

So, sweet Captain Kangaroo, farewell.

With love,
TERESA

21

"My mommy'll do it!"

What happens to a mother when all her children are finally, at last, enrolled in school?

I had so many plans for this particular day; for eighteen years I had been dreaming of all the things I would do when the kids were sequestered for six hours a day in a classroom. I would drive to the supermarket and shop, all by myself, with nobody to bounce in the basket, to pull packages off the shelves, to run through the aisles raising terror in the toy section.

Or I would drive to the shopping center and try on clothes to my heart's content, with no giggling toddler standing around, staring and saying:

"Gee, Mommy, how come you're so fat?"

Or I would drive to the bowling alley and join a team, or to the golf course or tennis courts. . . .

Drive? In what? As any mother of ten children learns, by the time number ten starts to school, numbers one, two, three, and four have drawn lots for the car, leaving mother at home to clean house.

Okay, so I'll clean house. At least I can do that in peace. First, the breakfast dishes. Why do they seem so dreary today? Is it because Captain Kangaroo isn't cheerfully chatting in the background and no excited toddlers are here to tell me of the latest antics of Bunny Rabbit and Mr. Moose?

No Captain Kangaroo. Say, that means I can watch the "Today" show.

This can't be the "Today" show. Where's Dave Garroway?

Better make the beds. Funny, making beds has never seemed like work before. It was more like a game, with one or two toddlers bouncing on the mattress, rolling and wrestling and giggling, entangling themselves in sheets and bedspreads, begging me for a tickle or a hug. And where is my laughing little helper? Following his new ladylove around the kindergarten, helping her pass out poster paper. Fickle, fickle child. How soon we forget our first love!

Say, did you know that it is possible to scour a bathtub without leaving a trail of scouring powder on the floor, the rug, the door, the hall, and the landing? But how can one clean a bathtub without first sailing toy boats or dunking rubber duckies? This is no way to work!

Back to the living room to pick up the toys and rearrange the clutter. What toys? What clutter? This place looks like a convent parlor; too neat, too clean, too quiet.

Quiet. Did I once long for quiet? No one shouting or squabbling, whining or crying. That's what I thought quiet would be. No one told me Quiet is no one laughing or singing, reciting rhymes and riddles, "bothering" me for a kiss or a hug.

I don't like this kind of quiet.

Which is a good thing, because there is another thing a mother of ten children soon learns. By the time Baby is off to school, his big brother is off to college. Except we live in a city where the college isn't far enough "off." Two hours after our baby went off to school, his brother came bouncing through the back door, shouting:

"Hey, Ma! What's to eat? Got any bacon and eggs? Okay if I throw these books on the sofa? While you're cooking, I'll read you my English report!"

Anyway, my car's back.

Oops, I'm sorry I said that. The homeroom mother must have heard me.

What happens to a mother when all her children go off to school? I'll tell you what happens to her. She goes off to school with all her children.

As recently as a decade ago my world was serene and secure, unscheduled and uncluttered with appointments or accomplishments. With eight children under ten, and the promise of more to come, I had nothing at all to do except rock the baby; feed the family; make formula, sweaters, mittens, and birthday cakes; wash dishes, clothes, windows, and tiny faces; clean high chairs, playpens, cribs, and closets; find schoolbooks, gym shoes, milk money, and Danny's glasses; write notes to teachers and letters to Grandma and lists for the grocer. But that was about all. Can you believe that I actually considered myself *busy?*

After years of such an easy existence, my carefree life suddenly went haywire, and I can tell you the exact moment this happened. It took place the morning Patrick, our youngest, went off to school, sat in his classroom, waved his arm vigorously in the air and said:

"My mommy'll do it!"

Good old Mommy. With everybody in school, what could she possibly have to do all day? No babies to feed, no diapers to fold, no formula to fix, no toddlers to chase. Mommy must be so bored, just sitting at home all day with "nothing to do."

Nothing to do. In a child's eyes, all the work that Mommy does (anyway, anything *important*) is centered around *him,* and if he is busy at school, Mommy surely must be languishing at home, anxiously awaiting his return. Why make her wait? Let's bring her to school!

Surely Mommy would just love to be Room Mother (Den

Mother, Teacher's Aid, Field-trip Chaperone, Playground Mother, Cafeteria Helper, Record Keeper, Car-pool Coordinator), and how can Mommy say No?

So Mommy gets active in the PTA and meets other Mommies who recruit her for parish work, or volunteer duty at the hospital, or just a little time on a political campaign or a charity ball, and as long as you are going to be out this afternoon, honey, would you mind stopping at the hardware store to pick up some pruning shears, and stop at the cleaners for my suit, and while you're at it I think the lawn mower's ready at the Fix-It Shop.

What happens to a mother when all her children get into school?

Who knows? Nobody's ever been able to catch one long enough to find out.

22

Resolutions for the new school year

Happy New Year!

I know it's not January 1. What's exciting about January 1? I celebrate New Year's the day after Labor Day, when the kids go back to school. Don't you feel sorry for childless couples who, not having spent a rotten summer, don't know the joy of sending the kids back to school?

As I have already sent off my instructions to the principal on BLOOMINGDALE'S RULES AND REGULATIONS FOR RUNNING THE SCHOOL, I now offer to all parents TERESA'S SUGGESTIONS FOR SURVIVING THE FIRST WEEK OF SCHOOL.

First, on the night before school starts, get to bed early, because you are going to have to get up early in order to have time to find all the things the kids swore they laid out the night before.

School sweaters? "We don't need them today; it's too hot." Make them wear them anyway; otherwise when it gets cold they won't be able to find them.

School shoes? He left them at the park. Why did he wear

them to the park? Why didn't he wear his tennis shoes? He couldn't find them. Do they let kids go to school barefoot on the first day? Sorry, it starts a precedent; there will be ninety-six more school days when he can't find either pair of shoes. So you will have to allow time to go by the park, or possibly the shoe store.

The kids? I know, they are right there. But all of them? Have you counted? (Good Lord. One forgot to get up!)

Okay, now you have found everything and everybody.

So the second suggestion is, Mortgage your home. Why do you have to mortgage your home? Because this afternoon your kids are going to bring home the Supply List, and you will need a zillion dollars for notebook paper, pencils, pens, scissors, glue, binders, pocket folders, compass, erasers, spiral notebooks, assignment notebooks, science notebooks, book covers, paper clips, rubber bands, lip gloss, mascara, and the latest Barry Manilow album.

These last three items appear only on the list of your eighth-grade daughter and you may question the fact that they are "required," but take my word for it, they are. Unless, of course, you are prepared to have your daughter "die of absolute shame and humiliation in front of the entire class."

A word of advice about the notebook paper: Do not buy five reams of the "On Sale" notebook paper on the theory that your kids will use it eventually. They won't use it *ever*, because none of its five holes are equidistant with the rings in the binders you bought. Also, the Supply List specified narrow-lined, and you just bought wide-lined. Why do you think it was on sale?

Despite what your first-grader says, he does not need the super-deluxe-jumbo-108-color-pak-crayons. The 8-basics will do just fine. You can invest in the 108-pak if you want to, but by next week he will be down to the 8-basics anyway because he will have loaned all the neat colors to the kids whose mothers were smart enough to buy the 8-basics.

Beware of erasers small enough to swallow, compasses sharp

enough to stab, and rubber bands thick enough to use as sling-shots. Buy the smallest bottle of glue; it spills just as fast as the big bottle and is cheaper to replace.

On the list you will note: Magic Markers, India ink, and oil paints. Ignore them, unless you were planning on redecorating your downstairs anyway.

This about covers the Supply List, except for the one item which I will explain in my third suggestion:

Buy yourself a megaphone. Having spent the summer sleep-ing till noon every day, your children cannot be roused at 7 A.M. with anything less than a mighty roar. Once they are awake and up, you will still need the booming voice to referee their pre-breakfast battles:

"Those are my sox; if you don't take them off right this min-ute I'll break your leg!" . . . "Somebody used my toothbrush! Ecchhh!!" . . . "Are you going to stay in that bathroom forever?" . . . "Gimme my hairbrush; I paid for that with my own money!" . . . "I dare you to hit me! I dare you! I dare you! I dare you! Mom! He hit me!!" . . . little things like that.

Fourth suggestion: Resist the temptation to delight your chil-dren with a first day goodie-roony lunch of special sandwiches, surprise salad, packaged puddings, et cetera. It's better to start out blah. You can always follow peanut butter and potato chips with chicken salad and chocolate cake, but you can't follow chicken and cake with a cheese sandwich and a celery stick. In fact, it is a good idea to stay away from the chicken salad and chocolate cake altogether. Kids spoil easier than bananas. Make them eat peanut butter.

Fifth suggestion: Do not, under any circumstances, drive your children to school that first day, no matter how anxious you are to get them out of the house. For if you do drive on the first day, you can be sure that on the second day they will scream: "Walk six blocks? You've gotta be kidding!" And by the third day, they will have assumed it is their constitutional right to be chauffeured. Furthermore, if you drive them to school on a lovely, warm, late summer morning, what do you think they are going to demand come February, with three feet of snow and a wind-chill index of 65 below? No, you have to start the year right: shove them out the door and make them walk. And don't watch; they will limp, drop their books, linger and loiter, in the hopes that you will change your mind. Don't worry about them; they'll make it.

But of course you will worry, as all mothers do, especially when a little child is going off to school alone, after a summer under mother's protective eye. And this is where the sixth and last suggestion comes in:

Rely on their Guardian Angels. Christians have always depended on Guardian Angels to "protect us, lest we dash our foot against a stone," and recently Billy Graham reminded us that *everybody* (even Idi Amin!) has an angel. (Wouldn't you hate to be Idi's angel?)

Don't get too lonesome for your kids. By next Monday, the teachers will have figured out a way to dismiss at noon, or cancel classes for the day, or send the kids on a field trip with you as chaperone. So enjoy your New Year's; because like everybody else's, it only lasts twenty-four hours.

As on the traditional New Year's, I make all kinds of resolutions once the kids are back in school. With quiet and sanity returned to the household, I take a new lease on life and promise myself I will inaugurate at least one project that would lead to Better Living.

Last year I decided to try for the Family Dinner. Come hell, high water, or football practice, the Bloomingdales were all going to sit down to dinner together, as a family, in the dining room. We had never really attempted this before, as it seemed we always had somebody in the high-chair stage, or at the age where they preferred fingers to forks.

But by last year, all the kids had reached the "age of reason," which, I assumed, meant they no longer had any reason to spill milk, smear mashed potatoes, throw tantrums, or throw up. So I invited them all into the dining room for a lesson in gracious living. We would have a linen tablecloth, glasses that match, enough silverware to go around, and some delightful, meaningful, intelligent conversation. We would share events of the day, and dinnertime would become an enjoyable, intellectual experience which all would look forward to with happy anticipation. I imagined teenagers rushing home from basketball practice in order not to miss a minute of our delightful dinner hour. Dates or other evening plans would gladly be postponed so that all could linger at the table, conversing, chatting, and laughing together.

Perhaps we would even borrow a page from the Kennedys and Buckleys and have a few minutes of French or Spanish conversation, as our teenagers were studying both languages. It was going to be a truly happy hour.

I must have been out of my mind.

It is true that the first word uttered, that first night at dinner in the dining room, was foreign. But unfortunately, it was neither French nor Spanish. To be honest, it wasn't even all that foreign. (I know I am conservative when it comes to the modern-day thoughts on freedom of expression, but there is no truth to the rumor that I slugged one of the kids last week for calling me Mother.) The "foreign" word, which floated across the dinner table that evening, sounded all the worse because it was uttered by our "baby," Patrick. He dropped a spoon, tried to catch it, knocked over his milk, and muttered: "Oh, f—."

"Patrick!" I cried. "Wherever did you hear that filthy word?"

"At the movies," he replied innocently.

"What movie?" I asked, knowing that the only movie Patrick had seen recently was a Peanuts Special, and somehow I couldn't imagine Charlie Brown . . . or even Lucy . . . using that kind of language.

"It wasn't in the Snoopy movie," said Patrick. "It was in the previews of a movie coming next week."

"We will forget what Patrick had to say," I announced firmly. "Does anybody else have anything to say?"

"Yeah," said Annie. "Make Danny quit doing that!"

"What's he doing?" I asked.

"He's swallowing!" she complained.

"Of course he's swallowing," I sighed. "He's eating his dinner."

"Yeah, but does he have to swallow so yucky?"

"That's 'yuckily,'" corrected her sister, Mary. "It calls for an adverb."

"Oh, Miss Perfect!" taunted Annie. "I suppose you never make any mistakes."

"One," answered Mary. "I was born your sister."

"Hold it!" I said. "This is not my idea of an intellectual conversation. Let's change the subject."

"I've got something to say," said Timmy, who seldom has anything to say.

"What is it, Tim?" I asked with interest.

"How come you let Patrick drink all his milk in one gulp? You never let me drink all *my* milk in one gulp!"

That about convinced me that the Family Dinner wouldn't work with the little ones at the table, so this year I tried a new theory. Three nights a week we would have a formal dinner, with only those sixteen and over allowed to eat in the dining room, they would "dress" for dinner, and I would make another stab at the foreign language.

The first night John came to dinner wearing his best slacks, with a tank top emblazoned THE ROLLING STONES.

"That is not what I consider 'dressing for dinner,'" I told him. "Go change your shirt." He did, and returned a few minutes later wearing a fishnet see-through with no undershirt.

"Try again," I said wryly, as the roast beef cooled on the platter.

Ten minutes later he returned, dressed in a tux. Somehow, I was more comfortable with THE ROLLING STONES.

As we finally settled ourselves to a cold dinner, I awaited the specifically requested intellectual conversation.

"Hey, Dad," said Mike, "can I have the car tonight?"

"Hold it," I said. "Have you forgotten, we are going to discuss intellectual topics at the dinner table? And remember . . . the language, the language!" Mike was in his fourth year of French; this should be easy for him.

Mike paused a moment, thought about it, then said:

"Say, Father, may I please have the car tonight?"

Before I could reverse the conversation, Jim picked it up: "Listen, idiot, you had the car last night. I gotta have it for the concert tonight." (God forgive them, they should call such noise a concert.)

"While we're on the subject of music," said Danny, "who stole the Simon and Garfunkle album out of my room?"

"Are you insane?" asked Mary. "Nobody in their right mind would go into your room. They would be asphyxiated."

"How do you know what my room is like?" shouted Dan. "Dammit, I wish everybody'd stay out of my room. Can't a guy have any privacy around here?"

"Look who's complaining about privacy," said Mary. "You have your own room; at least you don't have to share it with two sisters. And by the way, you guys, I'm taking the car tonight; I've got drama class."

"Nobody is taking the car tonight," their father finally declared, "unless they are prepared to fork over some cash for gasoline."

"I think that's about as close as we're going to get," I said quietly.

"What's about as close as we're going to get? Get to what?" asked my husband.

"To a foreign language," I said. "If there is any sentence that is foreign to this family, it is 'fork over some cash.'"

23

I'm listening

"How do you get your kids to talk to you?" my friend Sue asked me the other day. "My kids never say anything to me but 'What's for dinner?' and 'Can I borrow some money?'"

"I'll let you in on a secret," I told Sue, "one it took me years to learn. My kids talk to me because I listen to them."

"I listen to my kids," Sue said, "at least, most of the time, I do."

"Or some of the time?" I asked. "Or a small part of the time?"

Does anybody listen anymore? Listening is a lost art, as any observer of people can tell you. Watch a David Susskind panel discussion on television, or Bill Buckley's "Firing Line," which has fewer guests. Nobody seems to listen; everybody is too busy interrupting. On Susskind it is pandemonium; everybody talks at once, all the time. Susskind doesn't listen; the panelists don't listen; the audience *tries* to listen, but there's so much noise it's impossible.

Or watch the guests at a cocktail party. I say watch, because you sure can't listen to them; you'd go bonkers. Everybody talks at once. You'd think they were on the David Susskind show.

Someplace down through the years of watching Susskind and Buckley, and attending cocktail and dinner parties, I learned that it is much more fun, and certainly much easier, just to shut up and listen.

As I go to few cocktail parties, and watch little television, I soon found myself listening to my children. And I had to learn all over again not to interrupt.

Parents are worse interrupters than David Susskind's panelists. Our kids will come rushing in from school, shouting:

"Hey, Mom, wait'll you hear what happened at school today!" and we interrupt to say: "Go hang up your coat." So what happens? The kid goes back to hang up his coat, and you both forget about the school happening.

Or we interrupt to correct their grammar. My kids are "A" students in English (please don't ask me about science and math), yet they consistently use the double negative. I once discussed this with an English teacher at Creighton Prep.

"Mr. Spethman," I asked the gentleman who taught our son Michael, "how can you allow Michael to be in your Honors Course in English when he insists on using the double negative?"

Mr. Spethman thought for a moment and replied: "Mrs. Bloomingdale, I'm afraid I ain't got no answer for that." He was kidding, of course. (He later told me that he can't undo in a semester what television has done in a decade.)

My husband claims our son John hasn't spoken to him in four years. I asked John about that and he replied, "I'd talk to him, Mom, but everytime I start to say something, he asks me if I've checked the oil in his car."

"*Have* you checked the oil in his car?" I asked.

"I'll get around to it," he grumbled as he disappeared out the back door.

I don't know why he was in such a hurry; I was willing to listen to his excuses for not checking the oil.

If you want your kids to talk to you, let them talk. Don't interrupt to correct, criticize, or hand out chores. Just listen.

Admittedly, this can sometimes be rather boring, especially if your five-year-old wants to tell you, in detail, about this morning's session with Captain Kangaroo. Or if your seventh-grade daughter wants to read you the thirty-seven stanza poem she composed for the poetry contest. Keats and Shelley I could listen to forever, but not Annie. Our daughter Annie fancies herself to be another Emily Dickinson. Would that she were. Emily, as I recall, hid her poetry in her bureau drawer. Not our Annie. Before she has put the final period on the final stanza, Annie is ready to read aloud her latest composition to any and all who will listen. "Any and all" being me. And I do listen, and try not to look bored, or appalled, or amused, no matter how weird or goofy her poem may sound. It sounds beautiful to her, or she wouldn't be sharing it with me. The poem isn't important; the sharing is.

Children hesitate to initiate a conversation with their parents because, in their eyes, we are always too busy to talk.

"Dad's always got his nose in a book, and Mom's always on the phone" is their chronic complaint which is, of course, a lie. I am seldom on the phone, but when I am, that is the moment they *must* speak to me. If you want to engage your child in a conversation, call somebody long distance. The second you get your party on the line, you'll get your child in the front hall, signaling desperately for your attention.

If you are on the phone, and your child signals for your attention, for God's sakes, hang up immediately and listen. Do not, I repeat, do *not* try to talk on the telephone while simultaneously communicating with your teenager. The mere flick of your finger, or twitch of an eyebrow will be interpreted as "Yes, dear," and you may get off the phone to discover, too late, that

you just gave your son permission to take your car and his girl to
Las Vegas for the weekend.

Kids should be taught not to interrupt, but they should also
be taught *when* to interrupt.

The "when to interrupt" rule was brought home most effec-
tively by Sister Jeannette Kimball, R.S.C.J. (then Mother Kimball), when she was prefect of students at Duchesne College in
my boarding-school days. Every year Mother Kimball would
launch the school year by reading to the dormitory students
rules to be followed by well-mannered boarders. These rules included a comment on "how ill-mannered it is to interrupt." Perhaps to catch our attention, or maybe to impress upon us that
every rule has an exception, Mother Kimball would tell the following story:

"Of course, there are exceptions. For example, a student approached me in the corridor outside chapel one day when I was
involved in a conversation with one of the lay teachers. I knew
the child was trying to catch my eye, so I deliberately kept her
waiting, to impress upon her that she must not interrupt. When
I had finally concluded the conversation with the teacher, I
turned to the child and said:

" 'Yes, dear, now what is it?' and she replied courteously:

" 'I hate to bother you, Mother, but the sacristy is on fire.' "
Listen to your children. Your bathroom may be flooding.

If you really want to converse with your children, don't try to
talk to them in front of Dad, the other kids, Grandpa, or the
dog. For a truly chummy chat, approach your child when he or
she is alone in his or her bedroom.

How do you approach a teenager in his bedroom? And I do
mean *how?* Do you climb over the books, the boots, the records,
the guitar? Yes, you do exactly that, and hard as it may be, you
don't mention the mess. Not if you want to converse. If you
must comment on the clutter, do so with good humor. Peek over
the mounds of clutter and ask:

"Are we alone? Are you sure? How can you tell?" You will

get a laugh, and you may get your point across. Furthermore, you will let your child know that you are in a good mood; you are not here to scold.

I have a theory about teenagers' messy bedrooms, which is: Ignore them. When my grown sons were teenagers, they lived like animals. I ranted and raved, yelled and screamed, and accomplished nothing. Their bedrooms continued to be disaster areas. To my utter astonishment, they grew up to be as neat as Felix Unger.

So now I ignore their younger brothers' and sisters' bedrooms. Other than an occasional peek to be sure the occupants are alive and well, I stay out of their private domains. I neither trespass nor comment. As a consequence, my children and I talk about more important things than pop cans and gum wrappers, and we enjoy each other immensely. I only hope my switch in tactics doesn't produce six Oscar Madisons.

Part VI

Life'd not be worth livin' if we didn't keep our inimies. . . .

FINLEY PETER DUNNE, *Mr. Dooley in Peace and in War*

. . . . and that includes our kids.

Mrs. Bloomingdale in war and peace

24

My favorite enemies

Poor old President Nixon. I suppose it will be a hundred years before he is appreciated for all the good things he did. Personally, I will always be grateful to him for one particular administrative achievement: the compilation of his Enemies' List. It was not the enemies, but rather the list that intrigued me. What a marvelous idea! Everybody should have an Enemies' List. You could hang it in the kitchen, and every time you get mad at your spouse or your kids, you could glance at the list and transfer all that hatred to your Enemy for the Day.

Frankly, I have had an Enemies' List for years, and though I am constantly revising it, it seems the same old perpetrator hangs in there at the head of it.

My favorite, all-time enemy is, without question, the school principal. I have survived ten principals in my career as Mother-of-the-student, and I am convinced that each principal bit the dust for one reason: the half-day session.

There is nothing more disconcerting to a mother than to spend the Children's Hour (7 to 8 A.M.) dragging the kids out of bed, finding their clothes, feeling their toothbrushes, fixing their breakfast, writing their notes and refereeing their fights, and finally shoving them out the door, only to hear them shout:

"Don't forget; we get out at noon today!"

There must be a special place in purgatory for half-day principals.

Number-Two Enemy on my list is the plumber who promises to come on Tuesday, but neglects to mention that he meant the last Tuesday in December. He shares honors with the paperhanger who does half a wall and takes a four-day lunch break, and with the carpenter who teaches toddlers how to hold tacks in their teeth.

Other cherished enemies include:

. . . The doctor's receptionist who gives me, along with twelve other patients, a one o'clock appointment when she knows the doctor won't be in till two. Mustn't keep the doctor waiting, must we? Mustn't we? Why not? It would be interesting to see what happens to a doctor who is kept waiting. Does he self-destruct? Return his calls? Sign his insurance forms? It seems to me it would be a better world if the doctor's receptionist would schedule the appointments for three, knowing that the doctor will be in at two.

. . . Hospital registrars who demand to know my name, address, social security number, insurance broker, the balance in my savings account, and last night's bingo winnings before they will call anyone to stem the bleeding.

. . . People who ask me to spell my name two, three, or even four times, then say: "Thank you, Mrs. Bloomington."

It is not just *people* who make up my Enemies' List; it is also things and theories.

High among the Things I Hate Most are computers, most particularly the computer that sends out a dunning letter two weeks after I have paid the bill. It wouldn't bother me so much if the computer would send me a simple bill, stating simply: "Pay Now," signed: "A Computer." But it won't do that. It insults my intelligence by sending me a "personal" letter, auto-typed, of course, with obviously inserted familiar references to "Mrs. Bloomingda." This computer only cost a half-million dollars, you understand; you can't expect a cheap thing like that to have enough spaces for a twelve-letter name. Then, to add further insult, it signs itself with a flowery, always feminine signature like "Sue Slater." Non-feminist that I am, I would probably obediently respond to "Sam Slater," but I refuse to be intimidated by a snip of a girl. Sue Slater can just go soak her transistors.

Last year, for some unexplained reason, we began to receive a magazine which we had never heard of, hadn't ordered, wouldn't read. Like good, honest folk, we sent it back, with an enclosed letter explaining that there must have been some mistake; we hadn't subscribed to this magazine, but thank you anyway.

We never received another copy of the magazine, but for the next twelve months we continued to receive bills, followed by stern letters from collection agencies, and finally, a formal letter on expensive stationery from a New York Law Firm notifying us that they had been retained to file suit.

"File away!" I shouted to my wastebasket, as I dropped the letter into it.

While I was rather looking forward to being ordered to New York to stand trial (would I have time for a Broadway show or two?), my husband told me not to count on it, and as always, he was right. No subpoena arrived. There were, however, four more legal letters, each more threatening than the last, but the final letter was the real kicker. The attorney "regretted to inform" us that he must notify the magazine that we were ignoring their bill. Somehow this did not shake the subscription price out of me.

I was curious to know just how prestigious this law firm was, but when I went to look it up in Martindale-Hubbell, it wasn't listed. My lawyer-husband explained this to me. It seems computers, however legal, are seldom admitted to the Bar.

Also among my Most Hated Things are movies in which the middle-aged hero falls into bed with a twenty-year-old heroine. It's not the sex that bothers me as much as the age difference. Think about it. Do you ever see James Garner, Paul Newman, Jack Lemmon, Burt Lancaster, James Coburn, or Charlton Heston costarring with Doris Day, Joan Fontaine, Rosemary Clooney, Jeanne Crain, June Haver, or Ann Blythe? No, of course not. Paul Newman woos Kathryn Ross, while Charlton Heston plays pat-a-cake with Karen Black, and Burt Lancaster makes goo-goo eyes (thru bifocal contacts, no doubt) at Jacqueline Bisset. Meanwhile, where are Doris, Joan, Rosie, Jeanne, June, and Ann? Retired at middle age with memories of *their* movie lovers: James Stewart, Cary Grant, Bing Crosby, Dana Andrews, Fred Astaire, and Joseph Cotten. Frankly, I'd like to see a movie featuring a torrid love scene between Bette Davis and John Travolta. It would not only emphasize the fact that a May-December romance is just as ridiculous as a December-May, but it would be so much fun to hear what Bette Davis has to say about movie hero-heroines who fall into bed . . . unwed!

I also hate television commercials. Not the obvious ones picturing, in living color, the human body in various stages of nausea, constipation, congestion, or shampooing in the shower (Those I despise!), but rather the ones which send my kids rushing out to the kitchen, screaming: "Gimme, get me, bring me, buy me!"

These commercials are run every 9½ minutes during the Christmas shopping season, which now starts about the Fourth of July. You know the commercials I mean:

"Hi there, kiddies! It's almost Christmas! Ask Santa to bring you a Slippy-Slide Sled, and tell him to bring sleds to each of your brothers and sisters, too! You can have so much fun on your Slippy-Slide Sled. Only $99, plus tax. Slightly higher in states where it snows."

Or: "Ask Mommy to buy you a Busy Betsy doll. Busy Betsy walks, talks, eats, drinks, sings, swears, and ages before your eyes." (Mommy does that; who needs Betsy?) "Busy Betsy is only $9.95. . . . With clothes, $79.50."

Or: "Tell Dad you must have the supercolossal, custom-made, ten-speed racing bike with racer seat, psychedelic headlights, CB radio, night-sight mirrors, and removable training wheels. Only $495. Unassembled."

Among my Most Hateable Theories is Darwin's Theory of Evolution, and the Theory, proposed by an astronomer at the California Institute of Technology, that the earth is sixteen billion years old. (He apologized for his earlier error; in 1961 he claimed the earth was only ten billion years old.)

Darwin, as everybody knows, thinks we all descended from apes. Isn't that silly? I don't know where he ever got that theory, unless possibly he knew my friend Gloria's uncle Harry, who was the most well-named guy I ever saw. I'll admit there might be a remote resemblance between man and ape *physically*, but if you make a mental comparison, the theory is shot to hell. Have you ever known a monkey who was stupid enough to spend all Saturday afternoon hitting a little ball and following it around a hot, humid, hilly golf course? Or dumb enough to sit for four hours listening to Howard Cosell? Or sick enough to swoon over the Sex Pistols? I think Darwin should apologize to the apes.

As for the fellow who thinks the world is sixteen billion years old (or even ten billion; so what's six billion here or there? Nobody's perfect), the poor dear must be crazy as a loon because everybody knows the earth is only six thousand years old. How do I know? Because Mother Heydel told me so when I was in first grade. She told us Christ was born two thousand years ago, and the world had waited four thousand years for His Coming, and any idiot knows that adds up to only six thousand.

Of course, I realize that God could have created the universe, and then waited around awhile before He created people, but if He had first created the universe and then spent 15,999,994,000

years contemplating the creation of man, I have a feeling He
would have changed His mind. Certainly, He must have wondered, in the past sixteen billion or six thousand years, whether
it was such a good idea, after all.

A favorite Hate of mine is the theory that health, happiness,
and maybe even eternal salvation can only be attained by physi-
cal exercise, most particularly jogging twelve times around the
block in a smelly sweat suit at six in the morning. I have nothing against joggers, if they would just *jog* and shut up about it.
But they always have to brag, brag, brag. Like my friend Freda.
Every chance she gets, Freda tells me how wonderful she feels
because she got up at 5:30, did one hundred push-ups, and
jogged a mile before getting breakfast, packing lunches, and getting the kids off to school. Big deal. Anybody can do that. The
real accomplishment is to get up twenty minutes after the alarm
goes off, fix breakfast, pack the lunches, get the kids off to
school, and get back to bed without ever opening the other eye.
Try that for feeling wonderful.

Exercise is going to ruin the world; the modern generation is
going to grow up to be idiots. Healthy idiots, maybe, but idiots,
nonetheless. In the good old days, school kids spent five and a
half hours of the school day in the classroom, and half an hour
at recess, where they sneaked behind the gym and smoked
Camel cigarettes, like good, normal American kids. Now they
spend half an hour in the classroom, and five and a half hours
doing push-ups, lifting weights, and chasing each other around
the field-house track. Does this make them feel wonderful? No;
all it makes them is too pooped to empty the wastebaskets when
they get home from school.

I'm not against exercise, you understand. I'm just against exercise per se. Exercise per something, I'm all for. Why make a
second-grader spend valuable schooltime, doing knee bends
when it would be twice as beneficial to send him home to pick
up his Lincoln logs? Tennis and volleyball may develop shoulder muscles, but so does window washing. One of my sons

spends ninety minutes a day lifting weights. I've been waiting a week for him to lift the sofa so I can vacuum under it. Another son has to have a ride to school every day so that he will have enough energy to run the cross-country. And would someone please explain to me why a girl, who can spend an hour a day in a chlorinated, chemically polluted swimming pool, breaks out in hives if she submerges her hands in dishwater?

Currently heading my Hate list is the imbecile who is trying to commit the United States to the metric system. If the metric system goes in, I go out. There is no way, at my advanced age, that I can learn kilowatts and kilograms and meters and liters and grains. It took me twelve years to figure out ounces and inches and pints, and I still can't tell a bushel from a peck. I refuse, absolutely, definitely, and postively, to even *think* metric, let alone try to measure it.

But my children tell me that I must, for even though the government has not yet made it law, the school principal wants us all to learn, along with our kids, the metric system.

So guess who's back on top of my Enemies' List?

25

Rules for surviving your teenagers

The theologians are at it again.

Remember the good old days, when "theologians" were doctors of the church; wise, holy men who spent their time praying and teaching and explaining God's relationship to the world?

Today's theologians must have very little time for prayer and teaching, because they devote so much time to arguing. I suppose yesterday's theologians argued, but they had the sense to argue in Thomistic phrases which nobody understood, so we didn't have to worry about them. Today's theologians argue in everyday language that the common man can understand, which means, of course, that the common man gets into the argument, and that's what upsets the common woman. Namely, me.

I have spent the last year listening to my son, the scholar, carry on long-distance arguments with theologians who seem to be less concerned with God and His relationship to the world than they are with such issues as: Was Jesus an only child? Gee, I would love to be a theologian. It must be wonderful to have time to sit around and worry about the possible existence of Jesus' brother or sister.

As it is, I could save those theologians a lot of "thinking time" if they would just listen to my theory, which is: Jesus did not have any brothers and sisters, and the proof of this lies in the fact that He is responsible for coining the phrase "brotherly love." Anyone who has been raised in a family with two or more children knows this is a contradiction of terms. "Cousinly love" . . . "neighborly love" . . . maybe even "sisterly love" . . . but "brotherly love"? I just don't buy it.

As a mother of seven sons I have been observing "brotherly love" for the past two decades, and if this be love, let us have less of it.

Just last week I saw "brotherly love" expressed when Mike borrowed John's new jacket and left it back at the college dorm. No loving blows were exchanged, but there was plenty of loving language thrown back and forth.

At what age do brothers begin to hate each other? They certainly aren't born that way. When our two oldest, Lee and John, were toddlers, they were inseparable. One wouldn't go outside to play without the other. They ate all their meals together, broke their toys together, stole cookies together, drove Mother crazy together. They even slept together; no separate bedrooms for those two. They wanted to be afraid of the dark *together*.

When Lee started to school, John shrieked in loneliness and frustration, waiting impatiently for Lee to rush home from school to report on his latest kindergarten caper.

In first grade, Lee learned to read, and proudly read his pre-primer aloud to his enthralled little brother, who hung on every word. (And who commented not long ago, when asked if he wanted to see the George Segal-Jane Fonda movie, *Dick and Jane:* "Naw, I read the book.")

At ages seven and eight, they begged to be in the same Cub Scout den, joined the same baseball team, and cheered for each other at every game.

During their grade-school years they shared comic books and clothes and even complaints. If John had a horrid teacher, Lee sympathized; he had the same teacher last year. If Lee got punished for leaving his bike out all night, John sympathized. (It was his fault.) They shared a hatred of arithmetic, baths, and household chores, and a love of animals, bike hikes, and basketball. They even managed to get along with one basketball!

It was a beautiful relationship. It was also a temporary one.

The inevitable happened. Lee turned thirteen, and suddenly his twelve-year-old brother was a nuisance, a pest, a little kid! Why did he have to tag along all the time? Couldn't a guy ever have any privacy?

By fourteen and fifteen, John hated Lee for being older and bigger and a sophomore (who wants to be a dumb old freshman, anyway?), and Lee hated John because he didn't have as much homework, he wasn't expected to get a part-time job, and for cryin' out loud, what's he griping about, he doesn't even have acne!

The following year, at fifteen and sixteen, John hated Lee because now he could drive; and fourteen months later Lee hated John because now *he* could drive, and they must share the car.

They carried on a running battle over the use of the teenline telephone, the television, the stereo, the basketball, and their father's golf clubs. They taunted each other about the squeak in their changing voices, the speed (or lack thereof) with which their whiskers grew, the beauty (or lack thereof) of their respective girl friends, and their abilities (definitely a lack thereof) in driving my car.

In an unsuccessful effort to avoid the continuing conflicts, we sent them to separate high schools. John was a Preppie; Lee, a Cathedral kid. The traditional rivalry between the two schools raged throughout our household; the Jesuits haven't undergone such persecution since the sixteenth century. Amazingly, the Church survived; even more surprising, so did the boys.

When Lee graduated from high school, the screaming and the

shouting stopped. Busy with college courses, part-time job, and a new sweetheart, Lee was too preoccupied to pester John, who was stunned by the sudden silence. They shared the same dinner table and the same car, occasionally driving each other to work or school, but their entire conversation consisted of:

"How's it goin'?" and "Okay, I guess."

Then John graduated from high school and, to my astonishment, a real conversation took place between the two brothers.

"What do you think about the University of Nebraska at Omaha?" John asked Lee, who had just completed his freshman year there.

"It's an okay school," answered Lee, "but the courses are tough, and so are the teachers."

Whereupon, John enrolled at the University of Nebraska at Lincoln.

Then I blinked my eyes, and they did grow up. Now in their twenties, they have somehow dredged up the relationship they had as toddlers. They exchange ideas, lend each other money, ask each other's advice. On the rare occasions when they get together, they spend hours talking to each other. At least I think they are talking; I don't really know because I seldom have time to listen. I'm too busy refereeing the brotherly love amongst and between their eight younger siblings.

Thank God I have those younger siblings; they provide such splendid opportunity to apply all the theories I learned by making mistakes with my first two. For you cowards who stopped at two, I hereby offer you some Rules for Surviving Your Teenagers.

1. Buy your teenager an alarm clock. Of all the things he hates you for, he hates you most for waking him up in the morning.

2. When your teenager goes out at night, impose an exact curfew. "Come in early" will be interpreted to mean "early in the morning." Like about 4 A.M.

3. Never criticize the friends of your teenagers. The friend may be a real dud, but if so, say nothing. Your animosity will only strengthen the relationship. Keep silent, and your child will eventually drop the friend . . . who will, then, grow up to be wise, wealthy, and wonderful.

4. Never read your child's letters, notes, or diaries. You may be modern enough to accept the sexual fantasies, but you will never be able to stomach the grammar, spelling, and punctuation.

5. If you are persuaded to install a teenline telephone, do not put it in your teenager's bedroom (you will never see him/her) or in the kitchen (you will never see the end of him/her). Put it in the laundryroom. This will limit the calls to ten minutes, as no teenager can tolerate the sight of an upright ironing board for much longer than that.

6. If he/she drives your car, disconnect your gas gauge. They will never know how close the tank is to empty and will be forced to buy gas everytime they take your car. (Don't worry about running out of gas when *you* have the car; if you have teenagers, you won't ever *have* the car.)

7. If you can't stand the girl he's dating, tell him how sweet she is; if you hate the boy she's crazy about, invite him for dinner . . . with the whole family.

8. If you want your teenagers to read a particular book or magazine article, hide it in their father's "private, confidential, get-in-there-and-I'll-break-your-arm" bureau drawer. If you have something you don't want them to see or read, put it in the ironing basket.

9. For your teenager's peace of mind, don't ever go into his or her bedroom without permission. For your own peace of mind, don't ever go in there, period.

10. If your teenager threatens to leave home, don't say: "Fine, I'll help you pack." Your teenager will not only take you up on the offer, he/she will also want to borrow your best lug-

gage. Do say: "Okay, your little sister has been dying to get your room." (Caution: your teenager may *never* move out.)

Teenagers have one major fault; they eventually turn twenty, and then they are no fun anymore. They become studious and serious, motivated and mature, and horribly intolerant of their little brothers and sisters.

As one of our younger children said recently of her just-turned-twenty-brother:

"If there is anybody I can't stand, it's a reformed adolescent."

26

It's nice to see you again, too, Judge

"Look at that sweet baby boy!" said my friend Sue, as we watched a young mother cuddle her infant in the pediatrician's waiting room.

"What makes you think that baby is a boy?" I asked Sue. "That child is covered from throat to toe in an all-white pajama suit. No blues, no clues. It could be a girl, you know."

"Nope," said Sue, confidently. "It's a boy. Watch that right hand. See it clutching for the car keys? And the right foot; it's already stretching for an accelerator. That kid's not three months old yet, and already he's ready to drive. He's a boy, all right."

"Don't be silly, Sue," I said with a laugh, "that sweet baby over there in the pink smock is clenching her fist and kicking her feet. How do you explain that?"

"There are two possible explanations," said Sue, whose nine sons have two sisters, "that's a boy who follows nine sisters and his mother isn't about to buy a blue suit for one son, or it actually *is* a girl practicing shaking her fist at male drivers or, more likely, practicing stamping on imaginary brakes in preparation for the day when her own sons drive."

Having five sons of driving age, I will testify to the fact that all boys are born knowing how to drive a car. I discovered this the day I took our firstborn son for his first driving lesson. I had somehow managed to avoid that awful "learning permit," when he was fifteen, and had, in fact, procrastinated on the driving lessons right up to his sixteenth birthday. On that day I reluctantly took him out to the car, handed him the keys, and before I could fasten my seat belt, he had whizzed us out of the driveway and off down the street. By the time we had reached the first intersection he had persuaded me to accompany him to the Driver's Testing bureau "just to see if I can pass the test." Naturally, he passed with a perfect score, putting me into such a state of shock I agreed to let him drop me off at home and "go show the guys I finally got my license; I'll be home in time for dinner." (He got home in time for college.)

When I went in the house I asked my husband: "Where and when do you suppose that boy learned to drive?" My husband, who, despite his children's belief to the contrary, was once sixteen, looked up and said: "Do boys have to learn how to drive? I thought everybody knew how to drive."

No, everybody does not know how to drive, as I learned when I took our eldest daughter for her first driving lesson, four years and four older brothers later.

As Mary settled herself behind the steering wheel, she cautiously placed her hands on it and asked:

"What's this thing called?"

"That's the steering wheel, of course," I told her. "Surely you know what a steering wheel is."

"How would I know?" she asked. "I never got to sit in the front seat before."

"All right," I sighed as we fastened our seat belts, "start the car."

"How?" she asked.

"With the key!" I said.

"Oh"—she brightened—"do you need a key?"

I never know when Mary is putting me on, but I suspected that, in this case, her stupidity was sincere. So I began to patiently explain the step-by-step instructions for driving . . . and discovered her stupidity must have been inherited from her mother. I couldn't do it, and if you don't believe that, imagine yourself in the driver's seat. What is step one, two, and three? Ha! You don't know, do you? Of course not; we drivers don't know what we do, we just *drive*, for heaven's sake.

But I tried. "Put the key in the ignition . . . the ignition is that slot right there . . . and turn it."

"Okay," she replied, and proceeded to grind my starter to a pulp.

"STOP!" I ordered. "Try it again, gently."

"Now what?" she asked, as the motor purred.

"Put the car in reverse and back out of the driveway. . . . LOOK IN THE MIRROR!"

"I *am* looking in the mirror!" she said as she jammed on the brakes. "I can't drive like this!"

"Why not?" I asked.

"I forgot to put on lip gloss. You don't expect me to go out in public without lip gloss, do you?"

"Forget the lips and drive!" I said. "Just drive."

She drove. Back out into the street and right up onto the neighbor's lawn.

"STOP!" I cried again, before we hit their porch. "Put the car in DRIVE and ease gently back into the street." She did, and since I had neglected to tell her to TURN, we slid right back into our driveway, where I announced that the first (and last) lesson was concluded.

Eventually Mary did learn to drive, after an excellent course in Driver's Education, which probably explains why she is the only one of our teenagers who has never had to appear in traffic court.

Ah, yes, traffic court. I have spent so much time in traffic court the judge now calls me by my first name. The offenses, needless to say, were not against me, unless one can be ticketed for having too many teenagers on the streets at the same time, or even in the same decade. The charges were against one or the other of my sons, and as each was a minor at the time, he had to appear in court accompanied by one or both parents.

My lawyer-husband somehow convinced me that it would be unseemly for him to accompany our current convict, for, during my husband's career as a professor of law, he had taught the prosecuting attorney, all of his deputies, and possibly even the judge, depending on who was on the bench that day. My husband felt that they just might be prejudiced in his favor, which seemed like a grand idea to me, but you know how men are. I wonder what fathers who aren't law professors use for an excuse?

In any event, for a period of four years, I made an annual appearance in traffic court, a most interesting experience, the most interesting aspect being that I never, ever saw anyone I knew. This was unusual, as the tickets received by my teenagers had all been issued at a speed trap set periodically around the high school area. Each time the trap was set up, twenty or thirty boys were caught and ticketed, yet on the date of the court appearance, nobody showed up but the Bloomingdales. I soon learned that other parents simply paid the fine and punished their offspring in their own way, if at all. I prefer to let the kids sweat it out in court. Standing before a black-robed judge, listening to charges being read against you by a stern-voiced prosecuting attorney, can be an impressive learning experience for a teenage driver (not to mention his mother). Furthermore, a parent who has to stand in a stuffy courtroom, then lend eighteen bucks for a fine, then spend the next three evenings chauffeuring the criminal to traffic school, is not about to brush the incident off with a "See that it doesn't happen again." More likely, such a parent will be prompted to threaten: "If this happens again, I'll break both your legs." Or worse: "I'll confiscate your car keys."

Of course, the ideal situation would be to keep your kids on bicycles until they are old enough to buy their own car, pay their own insurance, and find their way to traffic court on their own. But every child learns to drive, and inevitably, every child begins to bug his parents to buy him a car.

Our firstborn son had not yet seen the sun set on his sixteenth birthday when he began to hassle us about a car. He argued that with an after-school job necessitating a two-mile trip every afternoon, he *had* to have a car; "nothing deluxe; just any old thing. I can fix it up myself."

The fact that our one and only family car was, itself, "any old thing," which he had never bothered to fix up even to the extent of emptying the ashtrays, did not in any way indicate that he was not sincere. I knew he loved cars and was an expert mechanic. Since the age of twelve he had willingly worked on his grandfather's car, his teacher's car, his buddy's jalopy, the neighbor's station wagon, and any auto he saw stranded on the highway. But he was always too busy to work on his father's sedan.

Still, I was sympathetic, and told him so. However, we simply could not afford a second car . . . and if we could, I certainly wouldn't indulge a sixteen-year-old child.

"He knows how I feel about kids who own their own cars," I said to my husband after the auto argument had raged for three days. "Why does he think we would even consider such an idea?"

"I'll tell you why he is convinced we will give in on the car," said my husband. "When he was six months old, we bought him a Taylor tot; at eighteen months, he had a teeny-trike, and at three, a tricycle. At five you gave him a scooter, and for his sixth birthday he got roller skates. A year later, his grandfather gave him a twenty-inch bike; when he wasn't riding it, he was on his skateboard. For his eleventh birthday we gave him a twenty-six-inch bike, and when he was fourteen he conned his grandfather out of a ten-speed. That kid has been on wheels all his life. I'm surprised he ever learned to walk."

I would like to go on record: We did not buy young Lee a car.

His grandfather did.

Once your teenager starts to drive, unplug the telephone. Otherwise you are going to spend every weekend night, for the next five or six years, waiting for the phone to ring and a frightened voice to say:

"We're over in Council Bluffs and I ran out of gas."—or

"I backed into somebody's car and the policeman said I'd better call you because you might freak out if he did, and would you tell him I do, too, have a driver's license? I just forgot it."—or

"I told the hospital nurse she'd better let me call you because you'd think I was dead and it's only a broken leg."—or

"Hi, Mom. I have the right to remain silent, but I thought I'd better talk long enough to call you; do you know how to get to the jail?"

Not many mothers get called to the hospital or the jail or even to Council Bluffs, but this does not preclude them from *expecting* such a call each and every time her teenager has the car. From the moment he pulls out of the driveway, her heart pops up into her throat and stays there until he pulls back into the driveway, five or six hours later.

Fathers are not so afflicted. They absolutely refuse to wait up and worry on the theory that if the kid is going to call, he (Dad) will have to go to his aid, thus losing a couple of hours' sleep; therefore, he'd better get some shut-eye while he can. My husband also argues the false theory that walking the floor and worrying does not bring a driver home safely, which is ridiculous. I've been walking and worrying for years, and I can't tell you how many times I have worried the kids home safely.

Oddly enough, I never walk and worry during the hours before midnight, which is actually when most accidents occur. It is only after midnight that I begin to fret, and as the one o'clock curfew approaches, I begin to catalogue the various catastrophes which could occur. I thus work myself up into a state of panic and stay there until my teenager has come in, peeked around the bedroom door, and whispered: "I'm home, Mom. G'night."

If he is not home by two minutes after one, I am not yet panicked, but I am exasperated. Where is that boy? He knows I like for him to be on time. Why couldn't he start home just a little early? Has there ever been a teenager who came in before he had to?

1:08. Exasperation is replaced by anger. I suppose he ran out of gas. Darn it, I told him to get the tank filled up. At least, I think I told him. But surely, he would check the gas gauge! Or would he? How could he be so stupid?

1:15. He didn't run out of gas. He would have called me by now. He had a fender-bender. If that kid backed into somebody's car again I'll kill him. Why can't he be more careful?

1:25. Why doesn't he call? If he was in jail, surely they would let him call! Why do I think things like that? He has never been in jail. I know why I think things like that. Because I'd rather he be in jail than in the hospital. That's where he is; in the hospital! It wasn't a fender-bender; it was a terrible accident and he's lying broken and bleeding, in some emergency ward! Is that a siren I hear? That's his ambulance! Should I follow it? Should I start calling the hospitals? No. I mustn't tie up the telephone. They may be trying to call me.

1:37. I never knew we lived in such a busy neighborhood. Thirteen cars have come down our street since one o'clock. It's silly for me to stand here by the window counting cars. I'll get into bed and wait. I can hear the car pull into the driveway; I'll see the lights. I never knew my hearing was so acute; I can hear cars a mile away. Where is everybody going this time of night? Why don't they all go home and go to bed? Why doesn't *he* come home and go to bed?

1:42. Car lights at last! But wait . . . no, it's just somebody turning around in our driveway. How dare they? There ought to be a law against turning around in the driveway of a mother whose teenager is still out in her car.

1:45. He's never been this late before. The telephone. It's going to ring. I know it's going to ring. And it will be police telling me to come down and identify the body. Please God, don't let the telephone ring. Maybe if I keep looking at it, it won't ring.

1:50. I can't stand this. I've got to find out where he is. Who did he go out with? Sally. I'll call Sally's house and see if she's home yet. But what if Sally *isn't* home yet and Sally's mother is waiting up looking at the telephone so that it won't ring? I can't do that to another mother.

1:57. Oh dear God, please let him come home. Please let him be all right. I'm sorry I said I would kill him. That was a terrible thing to say! And I'm sorry I said he is stupid. He's not stupid. He's a good boy. I don't care about the car, God. You can have the car. I don't care if it's a total wreck, if You will just let him be all right. If You let him come home safely, I'll never scream at him again. . . .

2:00. "I'm home, Mom. G'night."

"WHERE IN GOD'S NAME HAVE YOU BEEN?" (I know, God, but what did you expect?)

"Hey, Ma, did you forget? Daylight Savings Time? This is the last Sunday in October," he said cheerfully. "We get to set the clocks back, so I took advantage of that extra hour!"

"I know about Daylight Savings Time," I growled, "and on the last Sunday in October we set the clocks ahead!"

Or is it back? What's the old adage: "spring ahead and fall back" . . . or is it "spring back and fall forward"?

Is this spring or fall?

I've got to get more sleep.

Part VIII

Grandma told me all about it,
Told me so I could not doubt it . . .

How she lied!

Mary Mapes Dodge, *The Minuet*, from *101 Famous Poems*, compiled by Roy Cook, Contemporary Books

27

Perplexing parables

I don't know who the fellow is who was responsible for translating the Bible into its present-day vernacular, but whoever he is, I hope he spends a hundred quarantines in purgatory trying to explain the new "easy to understand" version to a bunch of children.

When I was a child, we read the Bible daily (contrary to the old legend that Catholics never read the scriptures), but it was true that we were discouraged from trying to "privately interpret" the scriptures. There was a reason for this, and it was not due to the medieval (or premedieval) language of the scriptures; it was because there are certain chapters of the Bible which *nobody* can understand.

I didn't realize just how confusing the scriptures can be until they came forth with the new translation that, they claim, "any child can understand."

Maybe the problem is that I am no longer a child, but the new translation is, to me, more complicated than the old. For example, I could understand perfectly how a housewife would sweep her entire house searching for a lost drachma; I mean, who knew what a drachma was? Could have been a diamond ring; or a coin worth a hundred dollars.

But as the translators have told us, the drachma was not a jewel or a coin of great worth; it was a mere dime. And who is going to believe that a woman would spend an entire day looking for a measly dime?

A parable I have always loved is the story of the Prodigal Son. Now I realize that parable has much significance today, with prodigal sons moving out and moving in all over the place, but the "easy to understand" translations raise a few questions in my mind. For example: What happened to the prodigal son, say, the next day? I mean, after all that wining and dining and kissing and hugging, wasn't the kid spoiled rotten? Did his mother have to poke him and prod him to get him out of bed the following morning to do his chores? Frankly, I'd be surprised if the prodigal son lived to *see* the next morning; if I'd been one of his siblings I think I would have killed that kid. After all, the brothers and sisters had been hanging around home for years and years, doing the dishes and emptying the trash, and guess who gets the fatted calf? The black sheep. Yes, I think I liked that parable better when I wasn't allowed to interpret it.

Another parable which confuses me is the one concerning the laborers in the vineyard. You know the one: the sixth-hour workers agree to work for one denarius, then they picket and protest at the end of the day when they discover that the guys who came to work at the eleventh hour are also going to get paid a denarius. Now, as a mother who has mediated many an argument about allowances, I can sympathize with the householder who says: "Listen, you guys, I'm the boss around here and what I say goes!" (I know that's a loose translation, but if you think that's bad, you should read the new Twenty-third Psalm!) What I find difficult to understand is: If the last shall be first and the first last, how did the householder ever again get anybody to come to work first?

A chapter in the Bible which definitely does not confuse me, but does stimulate my curiosity, is the story of the Child Jesus lost in the temple. As a mother who once left her five-year-old standing in the church parking lot while she drove off with his nine brothers and sisters, I am completely sympathetic with the Blessed Mother (though one would think, with only one child . . .), but I have often wondered how she explained the whole thing to her own mother? Now I am sure St. Anne was a perfect mother-in-law, but can't you just imagine what she must have said to St. Joseph when she discovered he had left her favorite grandson in Jerusalem? Knowing St. Joseph, however, I imagine he avoided that event by telling Mary and Jesus, on their return home: "Let's not mention this to Grandma, okay?"

I don't mean to be flippant about the scriptures; it's just that the new, informal translations seem to invite such casual commentaries. I don't really mind their making the Bible "easier to understand" (as long as they leave me an aesthetic Douai version to read and appreciate), but I do wish they would sit in on some of our family scripture-study hours to see what we modern parents must put up with.

For example, one night when we were studying Genesis, Patrick asked: "What was Cain's punishment for killing Abel?"

Before I could give the scriptural answer, Pat's brother Tim shouted:

"He suffered a fate worse than death; he had to marry his sister!"

The answer brought general hilarity (but no arguments), and when the children had calmed down I patiently explained that the scriptures state clearly that, after killing his brother, Cain was forced to leave home and wander the earth forever.

Whereupon our son, Jim, whose goal in life is to leave home and wander the earth, asked in astonishment:

"No kidding? Wow! What a punishment!"

I suppose there is little chance that those hard-working, well-meaning biblical translators will ever suffer in purgatory, despite what they did to my Douai, but I would certainly like to be in heaven the first time they meet up with King James.

28

My bad luck runneth over

When I retire I'm going to move to Albuquerque. I've never been to Albuquerque, but I just know that it's my kind of town. Why? Because they are loyal to their losers, and if ever there was a loser, 'tis I.

Remember the famous football game between Albuquerque and Las Vegas? Albuquerque lost, 100–0. No kidding; it was a real wash-out. My kind of wash-out: total. At the half, with Las Vegas ahead 61–0, both coaches agreed to play ten-minute quarters to alleviate the torture, but it didn't help. Las Vegas still scored another thirty-nine points. Total yards scored: Las Vegas, 565; Albuquerque, minus eleven. I loved it. If I had been there, I would have kissed every player on the Albuquerque team. I know exactly how they felt; I've been minus for years.

Like the Albuquerque football team, I try. I really do. But I can devote an entire summer's day to housecleaning—changing beds, cleaning closets, picking up toys, books, clothes, et cetera, vacuuming the living room, dining room, bedrooms, den—and by the time I get back to the living room, I have lost at least eleven yards. One would never know I had been there.

I can't win. At anything. Last month I spent half a day cleaning my refrigerator only to discover that it wasn't moldy bacon and dehydrated leftovers that were causing it to malfunction, it was the motor. It had died. I traded in the cleanest refrigerator in town.

The week before, I had gone to the body shop to pick up my car, which one of the kids had banged up. I paid the $235 repair bill (always, always, it's "just under" the deductible), pulled out into the traffic, and got hit by a truck, which, of course, had the right of way. Total damage: $248. (However do people know I have a $250 deductible?)

Last winter I went to a garage sale and was thrilled to find an almost new, very expensive, baseball mitt. What a buy! It would make a perfect birthday gift for our Tim, who had signed up to play baseball for the Christ the King school team.

When Tim opened his birthday presents, he thanked me for the mitt, and thoughtfully waited till the end of the day to tell me that "while it's a great glove and I really like it and everything, I can't use it."

"Why not?" I asked. "I know it's a little big, but you'll get used to it, and you will grow into it."

"I won't grow into this one, Mom," he replied sorrowfully. "My thumb's in the wrong place." It was a left-handed glove.

"What are you gonna do, Mom?" Tim asked.

"I'm going to give it to the school athletic department and buy you a right-handed glove," I assured him. Poor kid. Knowing how tight I am with money, the poor darling undoubtedly thought I might consider trading him to St. Cecilia's for a southpaw.

That was also the winter that I laboriously knitted a sweater for Patrick, and that thoughtless boy had the audacity to grow three sizes before I had it finished. He wouldn't have worn it anyway; I put the buttonholes on the wrong side.

I am a loser, and I have long been resigned to that fact. I am not only a loser, I am an expert at picking other losers. (There is no truth to the fact that they become losers just because I picked them.)

I picked my first loser in 1937 when I pressed my tiny ear to the radio and cheered Jimmy Braddock on to defeat. Did Joe Louis appreciate my help? Probably not.

In 1947, after spending three of my high school years rooting for the consistently losing Christian Brothers High School football team, I switched allegiance in my senior year (when I started to date a boy from Central High) and cheered the Central Indians right out of their state championship. As you may have guessed, the trophy went to CBHS.

That was also the year I saw my first Notre Dame football game. Ah, what a thrill! The famous fighting Irish! They had been making football history since the days of Knute Rockne; what though the odds be great or small, old Notre Dame had won over all . . . until I sat in the stands. I ruined them with one loyal yell, and it took them twenty years to recover.

In 1963, I wrote a fan letter to Bud Wilkinson and ended Oklahoma's brilliant winning streak.

In 1968, I, like many other football fans, watched a fabulous guy named Bart Starr play for the Green Bay Packers, then the top pro football team in the country. They immediately became the bottom team in the country, and I have no doubt that I was responsible.

After that I switched to basketball and chose the beautiful Boston Celtics as "my" team. I was sure that Bill Russell was a big enough man to weather my jinx, but he wouldn't even try. He saw me watching from the other end of the TV tube, and resigned in protest. After thirteen straight championships, the Celtics rode the caboose, due, I am sure, more to my devotion than to Russell's departure.

My most spectacular "achievement" occurred in the 1972 Olympics. Knowing my ability to jinx an athletic event, my children wouldn't let me watch the championship basketball game between the U.S.A. and the U.S.S.R. But on hearing some commotion in the last few seconds of the game, my curiosity overwhelmed me and I did a terrible thing. I sneaked a glance at the television set. You all know what happened. I threw the Olympic arena clock out of whack, the Russians were granted three extra seconds of play and won the game by a lousy two points. I fully expected the CIA to have me arrested.

My fame as a sports jinx is exceeded only by my reputation as a political Jonah. In 1960 I voted for the "sure winner," Richard Nixon. In 1964, I campaigned for Barry Goldwater, and in 1968 I saved the country from catastrophe by coming down with the flu. I was too sick to vote. I remedied this situation, however, in 1972, when I voted for You Know Who and brought on the whole Watergate mess.

In local politics, I was even more minus. In the 1977 mayoral election I campaigned for a friend and neighbor, a fine young Jewish gentleman who was one of our very competent county commissioners. He was running a very close campaign against an equally qualified candidate, a lady who had served on the City Council. You will be amazed to learn that the lady was defeated but, unfortunately, not by my candidate. Two weeks before the election a south Omaha grocer filed as a write-in candidate, and won. A devout Catholic, he claimed it was a miracle. Nonsense. I don't work miracles. I just jinx elections.

I can't even win on the parish level. When my children started school, I signed up as a teacher's aid, willing to contribute my talents wherever they might be needed, either in the classroom or in extracurricular activities.

Where did they put me? In the cafeteria. As cook, baker, menu planner, proctor? No. I was handed a dishrag and told I was on the clean-up committee.

At the scout banquet, I was taken off tables and promoted to washing dishes.

At the basketball banquet, I was promoted again. To Floor Chairman. This meant I got to sweep the floors.

So when the Altar Society asked me to be chairperson for their regular meeting, I knew what to expect, and I was right. I was in charge of setting up the chairs.

At the school talent show, while talented Mrs. Lemmers directed the performers and talented Mrs. McLeay directed the musicians, talented Mrs. Bloomingdale directed the way to the rest rooms.

I am not surprised that the principal and teachers question my abilities and intelligence. My children treat me as if I am not all there and act as if they wish I weren't. At school functions they introduce me as "Mumble-mumble," then ignore me for the rest of the evening. It wouldn't be so bad, except everybody else ignores me, too. I must have a forgettable face. Nobody ever seems to know who I am. I have had children in the same parochial school for years, but the principal, on whose carpet I have been called so often my footprints should be recognizable, still calls me Mrs. Morningside.

I don't know why I expect people to remember me. My own children aren't too sure who I am. On last year's registration forms, three of the kids spelled my name Theresa, and two of them misspelled my maiden name, which didn't bother me as much as the one son who couldn't remember my age so he put down "about 50." Now that can be funny if you are in your thirties, and flattering if you are in your sixties, but it's downright dismal when you are on the wrong side of forty-five, and "about 50" is staring you in the face.

After spending years as the nameless, faceless, aging creature in the kitchen, I was surprised and pleased last week when the PTA president called and asked me to particpate in the spring fashion show.

"Why, I would love to model in the style show, Stephanie," I told her. "I've always wanted to be asked. I know there aren't many short, chubby models, but at least I'll add variety to the program."

"Well, actually, Teresa," said Stephanie slowly, "we don't need any more models. But the committee needs lots of help, and we decided you would be perfect to baby-sit with the toddlers while their mothers are modeling."

At least that's better than the clean-up committee.

I hope.

You'd think anyone who has lost as often as I have would give up, wouldn't you? There is one place I have given up, and that's in entertaining. If Perle Mesta was the hostess with the mostest, I am, without question, the hostess with the leastest. I panic at the thought of giving a dinner party. Why should a candle-lit dinner for twelve put me in a state of terror? After all, I cook for twelve three times a day, every day. Obviously, it's not the quantity, but the quality, that does me in. If I could serve my black-tied and begowned guests hot dogs or chili at the kitchen table, I could manage without a qualm. But when it comes to cordon bleu or chateaubriand, I can't even pronounce it, let alone cook and serve it.

I could even do the linen tablecloth bit, with china, crystal, and silver, if the guests would promise to stay in the dining room and not wander around the rest of the house.

That's the problem. Before I would give a party, I would wander around the rest of the house, and all I would see were spots on the sofa and stains on the ceiling and how did the chocolate chips get into the chandelier?

I don't need an analyst to tell me when and where I developed my party-phobia. It was the first year we were married. My husband, then a law professor, asked me to entertain the dean and law faculty at dinner. Fine. There were only six or seven on the faculty; I could handle a buffet dinner for fourteen in our apartment. We had no babies then; I had quit my job; it would be a breeze.

Actually, it was more like an ill wind. I planned an easy

menu, which included potatoes au gratin. Now nobody had ever told me that potatoes au gratin should be parboiled before baking. Do you know how long it takes to cook au gratin potatoes that haven't been previously parboiled? *Forever,* that's how long. And it takes twice that long if your guests are patiently sipping martinis and manhattans.

Did the guests get smashed with all that booze? No. And for a very good reason. Though our cocktail hour dragged for two and a half hours, all stayed sober, because the same person who didn't tell me to parboil au gratin potatoes also didn't tell me that martinis and manhattans should be prechilled. *Nobody* drinks too many warm martinis.

None of the guests that evening were too surprised at my incompetence. Before our marriage, while my husband-to-be was still in law school, I had been secretary to the dean of the law school. My ability to miscalculate grades, mistype tests, miscount students, and misplace everything on my desk was known to one and all. In fact, the entire faculty was astounded when one of their most promising students wooed and wed me.

After that disastrous party, my talents as a hostess went downhill. We gave other parties, but each time I was a wreck. For weeks before each party I would have nightmares of horrible situations: The guests would come to the door and the knob would fall off. So they would have to go around back, where our patio would be strewn with debris, trikes, and toys. One night, before a party, I dreamed that my husband's boss tripped over a roller skate and broke his leg. Then I dreamed we sat down to my carefully laid table, and there was a huge jelly stain in front of the guest of honor.

My nightmares got worse and worse. Though I always planned to sequester the children in their rooms while we entertained, I invariably envisaged them disrupting our after-dinner drinks with horrid arguments, chasing each other through the house, in their underwear.

Nothing like that ever happened, of course, but I wasn't about to push my luck. We stopped entertaining at home. Now, when we have guests to dinner, we take them to a restaurant, or to the theater.

Last night my husband and I were invited to the home of friends for cocktails and dinner. She, too, has a big family, but none of the children were sequestered in their rooms. They were each dressed in their Sunday best; the boys took the guests' coats, and then served the cocktails. The girls served the dinner, silently and perfectly, then just as quietly cleared the dining room and did the dishes.

There were no spots on the sofa or stains on the ceiling, no sweat socks peeked out from the living room chairs, no toys cluttered the porch. The entree was delicious and as perfectly prepared as the cocktails which preceded it.

It came as no surprise to me when, after the dinner was over and the guests were chatting in the living room, the hostess announced that she and her husband were moving to Las Vegas.

That figures.

29

Chess, anyone?

There is a place in this world for everyone, even losers, and I have concluded that if I am going to be a loser, I might as well be an expert at it. This can be very admirable for a mother, to learn to lose consistently, especially if she spends the first twenty years of her life playing Uncle Wiggly, Junior Scrabble, checkers, and Monopoly with little kids who like to win.

In her classic book *Please Don't Eat the Daisies*, Jean Kerr claimed it is practically impossible for a mother to lose a game of Uncle Wiggly to a six-year-old. Jean never met me. I can lose at anything, to any child.

I am not only an expert at losing at children's games, I hold the record golf score at the Omaha Field Club (99 . . . for six holes), and Omar Sharif is seriously considering writing a column about my bridge hands. (Forty-four consecutive Thursday afternoons as dummy.)

Until last month I had tried, and lost, every game but one, and that was chess. For years I have resisted the game of chess on the grounds that it is much too complicated for an adult to understand. If one is to learn chess, one should start at the age of three or four, before one learns to read and write, because only a totally uncluttered mind can understand the complexities of queen's rook to queen's knight, or whatever that nonsense is.

My husband is an avid chess player, so when he discovered shortly after we were married that his bride had no intention of learning the game, he quickly produced a family of chess players. All of our children can play chess, having learned the game at the age of five, and they are now all experts at it. But none want to play with their father, for the simple reason that he always wins, and as we all know, children (of any age) cannot bear losing.

So, last month, in a weak moment of wifely good humor, I offered to make one more effort to learn the Royal Game. It was ridiculous.

Can you imagine a game where none of the pieces move in the same direction? Some go forward but not backward, some both, some can move diagonally but not straight, some vice versa, and then there are four horses which jump crooked.

"That's not a horse, dear, that's a knight," my husband explained patiently, but it looks like a horse to me.

There are turret-shaped pieces called rooks but some people call them castles, so you have to remember both names.

Then there is a bishop, which you would think would be pretty powerful, but evidently he's an Anglican because he has to bow to the queen and doesn't even have the influence of the knight.

I don't know where the pawns got their names, but I call them "kids" because there are so many of them and they are always in the wrong place at the wrong time.

I should object to the game on the grounds that it is feminist: the most powerful piece on the board is the queen, who gets to go wherever she pleases and God help anybody who gets in her way, while the poor old king may take only one step at a time and seldom gets to do even that.

If you must play chess, do not play it surrounded by pint-sized chess champs. It is very disconcerting to carefully ponder a move, slowly reach for a piece, and triumphantly check a king, only to have a ten-year-old mutter: "Too bad, Mom. You just blew it."

"You have to use strategy, Mother," advised my daughter Peggy. "Plan your moves in advance; you have to stay mentally five or six moves ahead of Dad."

I have spent a quarter of a century trying to keep up with him; now I have to get ahead? Impossible. After all, I am not just a wife and game player, I am also a mother, and as such, I learned long ago never to plan anything in advance. It's all I can do to figure out the *now*.

"You'll never win at chess, Teresa," my chess-playing sister, Betsy, told me the other day. "You want to know why?"

"Not particularly," I said, "but I suppose you'll tell me anyway."

"Wives never beat their husbands at chess," said Betsy, "because while the husband is taking forever to plan his next five moves, the wife is trying to figure out what to have for dinner tonight."

She's right of course. I will always be a loser. But since I am such an expert loser, cheerfully consistent, my kids all want to play with me, and my husband says I am his very favorite partner.

Which, now that I think of it, makes me somewhat of a winner after all.

30

A gift for father

I never know what to get my husband for Father's Day. I know I shouldn't have to get him anything for Father's Day since he is not my father, but the first year we were married he gave me something for Mother's Day (as a promise of things to come; boy, did they come). So I had to give him something for Father's Day, and thus we started a tradition neither of us has been able to figure out how to abandon.

In those early years, shopping for Father's Day was easy; he had nothing and needed everything. But as the years progressed, he accumulated all the socks, ties, and tools he would ever need or want, and the choice of a suitable gift became a real challenge, which was complicated by the fact that each and every year, after I carefully choose, purchase, and wrap his gift, he goes out and buys the exact same thing the Saturday before Father's Day.

So I don't know what to get him. It isn't that I don't know what he wants. He wants a new car, a three-week vacation in a monastery, a Republican Congress, and a credit card that self-destructs when touched by teenagers. What he will probably get is another pair of pliers.

This year I asked the kids what they intended to get their father for Father's Day, and Mike said:

"Nothing."

"What do you mean, nothing?" I asked. "Why nothing?"

"Because that's what he said he wanted," said Mike cheerfully, "and every father should get what he wants on Father's Day."

"Exactly," I said, "which means you had better get him something."

"But he said he wants nothing!" argued Mike. "If he wants something, why would he say 'nothing'?"

"Because he's a father," I replied patiently. "It's tradition. Whenever you ask a father what he wants in the way of a gift, he always says 'nothing' but he doesn't mean it. Take my word for it; he wants something."

"Yeah, but what?" grumbled Mike. "I haven't got much money."

"Then why don't you give him your services?" I suggested. "Offer to wash and wax his car."

"I already thought of that," said Mike, "and when I suggested it, he just laughed and said 'No thanks.' He claims that when I gave him that on his birthday, he later got the bill from Wally's Wash-Wax."

"That wasn't what bothered him," I recalled. "What got to him was the fact that Wally's Wash-Wax is in Lincoln and you didn't get back till 3 A.M."

"How about you, Peg?" I asked, as Peggy came into the kitchen. "What are you giving Dad for Father's Day?"

"I'm taking myself to the movies," replied Peggy.

"Explain that one," I said.

"I asked Dad what he wanted for Father's Day and he said 'peace and quiet,' which seems like a ridiculous request in *this* household, but I'm willing to do my share. I'm removing myself for the afternoon."

"Don't ask me what I'm gonna give Dad for Father's Day," grumbled our tomboy, Annie. "I'm mad at him."

"Why are you mad at him?" I asked.

"Because when I asked him what he wanted, he said all he wants is for me to be a good girl."

"And you hate being good, is that it?" I asked.

"No," she said. "I hate being a girl!"

"I know what I'm gonna give Dad," said Dan.

"What?" I asked.

"I'm gonna mow the lawn all summer and shovel the snow all winter," he replied.

"Big deal!" said Mary. "You have to do that anyway!"

"At least I work around here," shouted Dan. "I don't spend all day in front of the mirror painting my eyes!"

"I don't paint my eyes!" yelled Mary. "And I spend most of my day ironing your shirts!"

As the typical adolescent arguments rang through the kitchen, I escaped to the den, inspired. I had an idea for the perfect Father's Day gift!

I got out our tape recorder and two blank cassettes. My plan may take some time to prepare, but the results should be spectacular. I would make two cassettes, one for my husband to play now, while the children are still at home, to remind him that they are not always awful adolescents; sometimes they are lovable offspring. The second would be for him to play in his old age, when the children are grown and gone, and he is lonely for them.

The first cassette, to remind Dad that the kids are not always bickering beggars, took weeks to make. The second took about an hour. The first included:

. . . Lee and John discussing the advantages of a college education in preparation for a career.

. . . Mike and Mary talking and laughing at the kitchen table as they do their homework together.

. . . Jim and Dan in one of their endless and enthusiastic discussions of the Nebraska Cornhusker football team.

. . . Peggy, singing one of her father's favorite songs.

. . . Annie, reciting one of her original poems.

. . . Timmy, reading a list of all the chores he has done this week. (Timmy was born to please.)

. . . Patrick, telling one of his lengthy, impossible, hysterical, ridiculous reasons why it cannot possibly be his turn to do the dishes.

The second cassette, the one to assuage Dad's loneliness in his old age, was obviously much easier to make. It includes one or more of our children, at various times, saying:

"Say, Dad, can I borrow five bucks?"

"How come you yell at me but you never yell at him?"

"You like her better than you do me!"

"You're not fair, Dad!"

"All the other fathers let their kids take the car to school!"

"Would you please stop treating me like a child? You forget, I'm almost thirteen years old!"

"Daddy, the third grade is going to the zoo Saturday, and I told the teacher you would drive."

"Guess what, Dad? Our cub scout pack just elected you scoutmaster!"

"But, Daddy, if you don't let me wear mascara to school, I'll be the laughingstock of the whole eighth grade!"

"Daddy, when you were a little boy, did you ever get to meet President Lincoln?"

"Honest, Dad, when I asked you to chaperone the sock hop, I didn't know they were going to have Earl's Earbusters play."

"I don't know why you won't let me go camping with the guys; all the other girls are going!"

"Uh, Dad . . . uh, you don't happen to have any pull with the traffic judge, do you?"

"Daddy, can I talk to you in private? But first, are you in a good mood?"

Then just for fun, I made a third cassette for myself, a Mother's Day gift to me. It, too, is of our children, the sounds of our children, late at night, asleep.

Bliss.

31

Blahs and the biolator

"Why didn't you ask me to do that for you?" I asked my husband one evening when I found him vacuuming our bedroom carpet.

"Because the last time I asked you to do something for me," he said, pushing the vacuum sweeper under the bed where I hoped it wouldn't swallow up my slippers, "you snapped my head off and suggested that I was an incompetent, inconsiderate chauvinist."

"That wasn't the last time," I told him calmly, as I retrieved my slippers, a library book, a half-finished jigsaw puzzle, and a scarf I'd been looking for since Christmas. "The last time I was a perfect angel. The time I snapped your head off was in December of 1967, when I was nine and a half months pregnant, the schools had been closed for three days because of a blizzard, my sister had just called to tell me her husband was taking her on a Caribbean cruise, and you told me not to count on going to the New Year's Eve party at the club because you wanted to watch the football game. And I wouldn't have snapped at you then if you hadn't asked me to get up and change the channel."

"I'm going to buy you a biolator," he said, "so you'll know when you are going to be in a good mood or a bad mood and can warn everybody in advance."

A biolator, as you all know (and if you don't, congratulations), is a battery-operated calculator which measures our biorhythms, which, supposedly, control our moods. Simply by punching today's date (that is, the date you are doing the punching) and your birth date (no cheating; it doesn't help), you can compare the answers to a silly chart and learn if today or tomorrow will be lovely, lousy, decisive, derisive, creative, catastrophic, happy, sad, or better left undawned.

If there was anything I did not want or need, it was a crazy calculator telling me to shape up, or snap out of it, or get with it, because my biorhythms say I should. So I didn't get the biolator. My son Danny did. And now he follows me around asking questions, punching keys, and predicting my moods or, worse, contradicting them.

Like the day I was cheerfully working in the kitchen, whipping up a birthday cake for Patrick, who was sitting at the table reading aloud from a storybook, anticipating the moment when he could lick the frosting bowl. We were thoroughly enjoying each other in one of those rare mother-child moments of togetherness, when the Calculator Kid popped into the kitchen and announced in a voice of doom:

"Boy, you better watch out, Ma. This is gonna be one rotten day!"

Or the day I was enduring what all mothers know as "one of those days." I had been up all night with a sick child, had come downstairs in the morning to find the kitchen sink stopped up, found an overdraft and four forgotten bills in the mailbox, backed the car out of the garage and into a telephone pole, and gone back inside to enjoy a good cry when Danny came downstairs and said:

"Enjoy your day, Mom. It's gonna be your best day for the next month."

I have not yet killed this kid, but naturally, I am considering it.

For all of you who are thinking of buying a biolator to interpret your mother's moods, don't bother. A mother's moods are simple to interpret. All you need do is consider the circumstances.

For example, you can count on Mom being a real grouch if:

1. Somebody brings home a note from the principal, saying that school will be dismissed at noon the rest of the week.

2. The TV announcer breaks in to say that the Frank Sinatra Special has been pre-empted by Monday Night Baseball.

3. The new coat Mom just paid $79 for is advertised in tonight's paper for $39.95.

4. The baby in the family has just enrolled in kindergarten and the obstetrician calls to say: "By golly, you're right!"

5. Mom runs out of gas just twenty-four hours after she had the tank filled up and twelve hours after one of the kids borrowed the car "just to run over to the library."

6. Dad takes Mom for a quiet, relaxing weekend, without the kids, at the nearest resort hotel, and there is a convention of junior-high-school band musicians.

7. It's the morning of the day Mom is having twelve cub scouts in the afternoon, or the afternoon of the day she is having twelve dinner guests in the evening, or the evening she was going to get to bed early but somebody has to be picked up from a basketball game at 11:30. (Of course Dad will pick up the somebody, but who will wait up for Dad?)

8. The dentist's office calls to remind of a four o'clock appointment, and the appointment is Mom's.

9. The high school sends home a note announcing that "The Senior Class is planning a field trip to the mountains and all your child needs is $75 for equipment."

10. It's Mom's birthday, and everybody forgets; unless of course, it's the fortieth birthday, which everybody remembers.

On the other hand, you can bet that Mother will be a veritable bundle of joy if:

1. Her eight-year-old comes home in tears because "we elected room mothers today and you didn't get it!"

2. The four-year-old neighbor asks Mom: "Did you go to school with my Mommy?" (. . . and his Mommy is twenty-five.)

3. The MasterCharge bill arrives and reads: "Nothing due."

4. Mom keeps her dental appointment and discovers the dentist broke both his arms.

5. The television set goes on the blink the day of the Rock-Around-the-Clock telethon.

6. Parent-Teacher conferences were last night, and Mom forgot to go.

7. The school assesses a $20 graduation fee and daughter says: "I already paid that out of my baby-sitting money."

8. High-school son comes home and complains that he got cut from the football team.

9. The grade school announces that the Christmas program will be a colorful pageant with an all-school cast, and the school will supply the costumes.

10. It's a holiday weekend, and the refrigerator chills, the stove heats, the sink drains, the air conditioner cools, and the weather is sunny, cool, and clear. (I know, I know. But isn't it fun to fantasize?)

Every family would like to have Mother in a good mood all the time, but of course that's unrealistic; nobody is in a good mood all the time, though Moms come closer to it than most.

However, if you would like to try for the all-time, 100 percent good-mood Mom, follow three simple suggestions:

Be loving.

Be quiet.

Be there.

32

Just an "average" mother?

Humorist Erma Bombeck once commented that she is haunted by a fear that she will wake up one morning and discover she is "just average."

I wish I would wake up some morning and discover that I am average; I have been trying to attain that enviable status for years.

I used to think I was average; I really did. I went to school, dated, fell in love, got married, had babies (I know it seems incredible, children, but in those days it was quite common for lovers to marry and produce children), changed diapers, picked up toys, joined the PTA, den-mothered cub scouts and Blue Birds, and even launched a little career. I was an average, normal wife and mother. Right?

Wrong.

How do I know? Because my children, the Experts, keep telling me so.

Not my little children. My little children are wonderful, and, aside from the fact that they keep losing their shoes and wash only the palms of their hands, they are perfect, if for no other reason than they think that I am perfect. No, it is my teenagers who despair of me.

According to my teenage daughters, I am not only subaverage and below the norm, I am also weird, gross, and impossible. Why can't I be like Julie's mother?

You know Julie's mother. Yes, you do. She's the one who drives to the PTA meeting in her Mercedes-Benz (because Julie's dad has the Cadillac), dressed in something by Dior, with her still-blond, naturally curly hair looking silky, sexy, and superfluous because, with her figure, who looks at her hair? Julie's mother, according to my daughter, lets Julie have her own room, her own telephone, and her own way, and allows fifteen-year-old Julie to date seven nights a week, with a midnight curfew on school nights and a Monday-morning curfew on weekends.

If my daughter had her way, I would not only look like Julie's mother, I would also cook like Julia Child, allot allowances like Rose Kennedy, sew like Edith Head, write like Jean Kerr, enjoy Jean's celebrated status as lecturer, playwright, and frequent guest on the "Tonight" show, all the time being, of course, readily available in the kitchen to put together a pizza or bake a batch of cookies.

In one aspect, at least, I do not disappoint them. I am always available in the kitchen, if not cooking or baking, then cleaning up after someone who did.

My sons are not so demanding of me. Being male chauvinists, one and all, they care not a whit for my career; all they ask is that I fulfill the tasks of the average mother, like, for example, teaching their little brother how to tie his shoes.

I admit, I was embarrassed that Patrick went off to kindergarten in slip-ons because he had not yet mastered the art of tying his shoes, and I take full blame. I had never taught him how.

Why?

In the first place, Patrick is left-handed, and it is very difficult for a right-handed mother to teach a left-handed child how to tie his shoes. And in the second place, Patrick is our tenth child, and frankly, I was up to here with teaching kids how to tie their shoes.

The same goes for telling time. Our college-age sons were horrified to discover, several weeks ago, that their three youngest siblings could not tell time. Again, there is a good reason for this, and despite what you are thinking, it is not that their mother is tired of teaching kids about big hands and little hands and half-pasts and quarter-tos, even though she is. The fact is, our three youngest children cannot read a conventional clock because we have no conventional clocks.

After the tornado of '75 destroyed our house and everything in it, we had to refurnish completely, everything from beds to brooms, towels to teaspoons, and that included, of course, clocks.

In the good old days, when our older children were little, clocks had two hands, twelve numbers, and little lines between the numbers. Teachers taught kindergartners about The Little Hand and The Big Hand; game makers produced toys that went ticktock and told the reason why; children's books, in prose or rhyme, taught toddlers about hours, minutes, and seconds, as well as how to set the alarm so Mama will wake up at midnight.

By 1975, conventional clocks were passé, and while we were not aware of it at the time, all the new clocks we purchased were either digital, abstract, or aesthetic. As for the digital, you don't have to tell time; it tells you the time. Our abstract clock has two hands and four dots; try to explain that to a toddler. And our aesthetic timepiece is a picture of London, with historical landmarks indicating the A.M. or P.M. hours. Even I can't figure out what time it is when the saber is pointing toward Buckingham Palace and the sword is aimed at the Thames.

So my sons complain that I won't teach the little ones to tie their shoes or tell time, but they would forgive me that if I would "just dress the girls decently." I do dress my daughters decently, but their brothers complain that "they look like something out of the 1950s."

The reason my daughters dress in the fashion of the '50s is because the clothes they wear were bought in the '50s. Like most daughters who have reached adult size, they "borrow" their mother's clothes, not realizing that most of my clothes are, to put it mildly, a bit outdated. Good, but outdated. In those days, clothes were made to last, and they certainly did, due to the fact, no doubt, that for twelve of those twenty years they were stored in the closet because their owner was constantly clothed in maternity smocks.

Like all mothers-of-many, I cannot afford to be fashion conscious. The family clothes budget barely covers the blue jeans and sweat shirts, little boys' shoes and big girls' sweaters. Mama must wear what is available, and if my daughters don't mind looking outdated, they are welcome to borrow my plaid skirts, loafers, and conventional cardigans.

So I admit that I am neither normal nor average, but this is not because I am different from other mothers, it is simply because I am aging, that awful accident which afflicts all mothers eventually—except, of course, Julie's. As we age, we change, not only in looks, but in attitudes and opinions.

This fact was pointed out to me recently when our adult children were at home for the holiday weekend, reminiscing to their younger brothers and sisters as to "how tough we had it when we were little" as compared to "how easy you guys have it." Our middle children immediately refuted that theory, and offered in argument their version of How Mother Reacts to a Situation when it concerns (a) the oldest child, (b) the middle child, and (c) the youngest child.

SITUATION: The child comes home from school, wailing that the teacher punished him for something he didn't do, screamed at him, sent him to the principal, and ordered him to copy two pages of the dictionary.

Mother's reaction to (a): "How dare that teacher treat you

like that! I shall report her to the school board and have her reprimanded immediately!"

To (b): "So? What am I supposed to do about it? You can just figure that's punishment for something you got away with last week."

To (c): "Forget it, honey. Your teacher is probably just getting old and tired." (Teacher is twenty-two; guess who's getting old and tired?)

SITUATION: Child comes home from school to announce that he has just joined the grade-school baseball team.

Mother's reaction to (a): "Wonderful! I'll reschedule dinner so we can all go watch your games!"

To (b): "Now what did you go and do that for? I suppose I'll have to join another carpool!"

To (c): "That's what you think. Forget it."

SITUATION: Child has just fallen off his bicycle and smashed his head against the curb.

Mother's reaction to (a): "Oh, darling! Are you hurt? Don't move. I'll call an ambulance!"

To (b): "Take an aspirin and go lie down."

To (c): "Did you hurt the bike?"

SITUATION: Child announces that he must have new gym shoes for school.

Mother's reaction to (a): "Of course, dear. Be sure to buy Adidas. And get two pair, so you'll have a spare."

To (b): "Again? I just bought you a pair three years ago! Here's $5.00; go to the discount store, and get them a size too big so you can wear them next year."

To (c): "For a half-hour gym class I'm supposed to buy shoes? Borrow your brother's."

SITUATION: It snowed all night and there is a three-foot drift in the driveway.

Mother says to (a): "Honey, I hate to wake you, but if you get up and shovel I'll pay you $10."

To (b): "Get your lazy self out there and shovel that driveway! I'll pay you fifty cents an hour, but don't dawdle!"

To (c): "What pay? You eat here, don't you?"

SITUATION: Child has just turned sixteen and wants to discuss the problem of transportation.

Mother's reaction to (a): "Since you'll have to get from school to part-time job, I suppose we should buy you a car. What kind would you like?"

To (b): "What's the matter with your ten-speed? No parking problems, no gas, no insurance . . ."

To (c): "There is nothing healthier than a good, brisk walk!"

SITUATION: Child is preparing to enroll in college:

Mother says to (a): "Off to college at last! Where would you like to go? Harvard? Stanford? MIT?"

To (b): "You'll love State U."

To (c): "Say, sweetheart, have you ever thought about joining the Army?"

Mother's reaction to (a) (b) (c) twenty years later: "I can't understand how you are all so different, when we raised you all exactly the same."

33

Don't blame me!

"What's a peacemaker?" asked Annie one day as she was studying her catechism at the kitchen table.

"What do you mean, 'peacemaker'?" I asked, not realizing she
was studying the Beatitudes.

"Christ said: 'Blessed are the peacemakers, for they shall be
called the children of God.' I am one of God's children; does
that mean I'm a peacemaker?"

"That's not what that means, dummy," interjected her
brother, Dan. "Christ meant professional peacemakers, guys
who run all over the world preventing wars and stuff, like the
Secretary of State. He didn't mean dumb old girls!"

Who says? As I dwell on that particular Beatitude, I think
perhaps us old girls are precisely whom Christ did mean when
He said "Blessed are the peacemakers," for if ever there were
makers of the peace, we are they.

A mother becomes a peacemaker even before she becomes a
mother, in fact, before she becomes a bride. She realizes the
need for her mediating talents when she first begins to plan her

wedding and the church becomes a problem. Her fiancé wants to be married in the college chapel, which is 150 miles from the parish church her parents have picked for the nuptial service. Of course the bride makes the plans, but only after she makes the peace.

Her preparation for peacemaking continues as she learns she is about to become a mother, and she becomes mediator between her husband and her obstetrician.

"You can tell that doctor of yours . . ." her husband will say, as she leaves the house for her visit to the doctor, during which the doctor will mutter: "You can tell that husband of yours . . ." Peacefully, she neglects to mention either conversation.

Mother becomes a professional peacemaker, not on the birth of her first child, but on the birth of her second, shortly after which the firstborn will begin to question the reason for the second-born.

"Why did you have a baby? Who needs him? Wasn't I enough?" The winds of war blow stronger as the children grow older, and battles rage over such issues as "Who owns the teddy bear?" and "Why is his ice-cream cone bigger than mine?"

The domestic battles are easy compared to the foreign wars. When her toddlers are finally old enough to play outside, the first thing they do is involve themselves in a neighborhood dispute, or maybe even cause one. Regardless of who was the attacker and who the attacked, Mother the Peacemaker assumes all guilt, murmuring: "It's my child's fault. I will punish him immediately," even if it wasn't, and she won't.

Mother becomes a full-time peacemaker when the child starts to school, and Mom must plea-bargain with "unfair" teachers, "prejudiced" principals, gym instructors who make her child "play too hard," and football coaches who won't let him play at all. Her peacemaker role is complicated and compounded if she has two or more children close in age, especially when the blue jeans are all the same size, and all marked "Lee's."

Mother is often frustrated in her role as peacemaker, especially when she must mediate between her children and their father. These battles rage the fiercest over the simplest topics: Who took the comb out of Dad's bathroom? The pliers out of Dad's workshop? The silence from Dad's Sunday afternoon? But as peacemaker, Mother understands why the simple battles must take their toll so that neither warrior has any strength left to fight the unwinnable wars, such as: How did he wreck the car? Why did he drop out of college? Who said he could move into his own apartment?

Mother's role as peacemaker comes full cycle the day her daughter announces that she wants to be married, in the college chapel, miles from home, and her father tells her he will give his blessing when the marriage takes place in her home-parish church. Then, and only then, can Mother-the-Peacemaker relinquish her title of Mother Mediator to the next generation.

The Beatitudes are not the only scriptural references to the responsibilities and rewards of motherhood; the Spiritual and Corporal Works of Mercy, which were written for all, are most aptly performed by mothers, every day, all day, for all of our lives. Just think about them:

To admonish the sinner: "Don't hit your sister." . . . "You must not talk back to the teacher." . . . "Careless drivers become car-less drivers!"

To counsel the doubtful: "Certainly, there are angels, and you have one of your very own." . . . "No, there are no such things as monsters." . . . "Of course you can learn algebra; just keep trying!" . . . "God will let you know what He wants you to be when you grow up; just keep praying!"

To instruct the ignorant: Everything from teaching a baby to walk and talk to teaching the teenagers to think and do.

To comfort the sorrowful: "Don't cry, sweetheart; we'll find your teddy bear." . . . "I'm sorry we have to move, too, honey, but you'll learn to like your new school, and you'll make new friends." . . . "There'll be other parties, honey." . . . "Sure we'll miss him, but just think what a wonderful time Grandpa is having in heaven!"

To bear wrongs patiently: "I know you didn't mean to hurt me; I'm glad you're sorry; now let's forget it." . . . "We are all unjustly criticized at times; offer it up to Our Lord."

To forgive all injuries: "Seventeen-year-olds seldom die of a broken heart, and the fastest way to forget is to forgive."

To pray for the living and the dead: "Say an extra Hail Mary for Mrs. Callahan's baby; he is very ill." . . . "Okay, kids, let's all pray your brother passes his senior comps." . . . "This week, we'll ask Father to say a Mass for Grandpa."

To give drink to the thirsty: The middle-of-the-night drinks of water to tiny toddlers . . . The gallons and gallons of lemonade on hot summer days . . . After-school cocoa on cold winter afternoons.

To clothe the naked: Everything from changing the diapers to choosing the trousseau.

To ransom the captive: Library fines . . . bubble-gum fines . . . traffic fines . . . votive lights!

To shelter the homeless: Taking care of the neighbor's children while their mother is ill . . . Welcoming back those young adult children who left home and want to return.

To visit the sick: Walking a colicky baby . . . Sitting beside a fever-ridden toddler . . . Holding the hand of a hurting child . . . Holding the head of an intemperate teenager.

To bury the dead: Teaching the toddlers that death is the doorway to heaven . . . Taking them to Grandpa's funeral . . . Emphasizing the beginning of Eternal Life, rather than the end of life on earth.

To feed the hungry (The Work of Mercy which guarantees every mother a free ticket to heaven): Nursing the baby; the battle of the bottle; strained spinach and all that spitting; the trauma of finger-food and self-feeding; the thousands of meals; unceasing snacks; sack lunches; picnics; parties; and ad infinitum: peanut butter and jelly sandwiches.

Mothers are marvelous creatures, and it's about time the world realizes that fact. If not the world, at least the kids. Our children don't appreciate, or even acknowledge, our talents and our virtues, because they are so obsessed with our faults and our foibles or, anyway, with the faults and foibles which they claim are ours.

Just the other day my son John said: "Mom, just look at all your generation is responsible for: the Depression, a world war, Korea, Vietnam, and Watergate. What a mess you left for us."

"Hold it!" I said. "You forgot the Cuban Crisis and the Kennedy assassinations, and just for the record, I haven't left, yet! By the way, I don't mind taking the blame for the atom bomb, the Pueblo incident, and the fact that John Dean's a fink, but you can hardly blame the Crash of '29 on a gal who was, in '29, not yet a gleam in her father's eye. And if I must take responsibility for the entire twentieth century, I expect due credit for the invention of the automobile, the airplane, radio-television, satellites, and the Salk vaccine. Any more remarks, Big Mouth?"

"Yeah"—he grinned—"what's for dinner?"

"Crow," I replied.

For all Big-mouthed children everywhere, I would like to clear up the following points: despite general claims to the contrary, mothers are not responsible for:

. . . . War, taxes, or the rising cost of Coca-Cola.

. . . . Multiplication tables, college entrance exams, acne, or Alice Cooper.

. . . . The gasoline shortage.

. . . . Car fenders that collapse at the gentle touch of a telephone pole. (Especially if, at the time of the gentle touch, Mother is standing at the kitchen stove.)

. . . . President Carter's foreign policy; President Carter's relatives; President Carter's cabinets (. . . including Ham Jordan).

. . . . Sunday sermons that last twenty-five minutes; church bazaars that conflict with the Super Bowl; the scarcity of cute girls at the 12:15 Mass.

. . . . Presidential press conferences which pre-empt football games, "Happy Days," or the "Bee Gee Special." (We are certainly not responsible for the Bee Gees.)

. . . . Telephones which don't ring when daughter's expecting a call, but do ring when Dad's taking a nap.

. . . . The scarcity of college scholarships; compulsory attendance at college convocations; $25 textbooks.

. . . . Little brothers who like to tease; big brothers who like to taunt; sisters who won't stand for either one.

Actually, mothers are responsible for the little brothers and the big brothers and all-size sisters, if not for their faults, most certainly for their existence. But that's not our fault. It's our virtue.

Epilogue: *The best is yet to be*

"Would someone please explain to me," wailed our teenage daughter the other day, as she was poring over her textbooks, "why they say that our high-school years are the best years of our lives?"

Why *do* they say that? Adolescence is so obviously the worst time in anybody's life, what with algebra and acne and the awfulness of growing up. I can remember how terrible it was, and I can still hear the grown-ups saying the same thing to me: "Enjoy yourself now; this is the best time of your life."

The only one who never said it was my father. My dad was the happiest man I ever knew, yet he frequently groaned about his high-school days. He had hated school (though he loved learning) and claimed he did not find true happiness until he married Mama.

When I would bemoan the agonies of my own adolescence, at age sixteen or so, my father would say:

"Cheer up, sweetheart, the best is yet to be!"

Wisely, Daddy never told me when "yet to be" would be. But

I soon found out. It was when I was seventeen. The acne and algebra were past and passed, and replaced by dances, parties, and proms, and a superiority complex compulsory for every high-school senior. Surely, her seventeenth summer is the best time in any girl's life. Or so I thought. . . .

Until I turned eighteen and went away to college. After the rigid discipline of convent high school, college life was terrific, even in a convent boarding school. In those glorious "between wars" years, we worried little about classes or careers; we were more interested in dorm pranks and dances, picnics, and frat parties. For me, college was four years of fun, late-night girl talks anticipating weekend boy talks, falling in and out of love, doing a little studying only if it was absolutely necessary. They were happy years; the best time. Or so I thought. . . .

Until I graduated. Grown-up at last! Free and independent, I had the ideal job. I was secretary to the dean of Creighton University Law School, where I was surrounded each day by several hundred interesting, intelligent, and extremely eligible young men. My date book runneth over; what a wonderful time; the best . . .

Until I fell in love. Ah, this is it! The wonderful courtship; the beautiful wedding; the rapturous honeymoon; the happiness which comes only to newlyweds. Surely, the first year of marriage is the best time. . . .

Until the babies come! I must be a "baby person," for, to me, there was nothing more fun or fulfilling than cuddling a tiny baby, watching him smile, listening to her coo . . . unless it was hugging toddlers who followed me faithfully, cheerfully chatting, adoring and adorable. Sometimes, during those years, I would sneak into the nursery and look at my sleeping little ones and just *know* that "this is the best time." Or so I thought. . . .

Until each child in turn made his or her First Communion. Glory be, what a change! In one morning, a little dickens would become a little angel. Suddenly, a toddler turned into a child, one who was now old enough to talk to and teach, to discipline and guide, yet still young enough to hug. Could that be the best time? I thought so, until . . .

They became teenagers; young adults. What marvelous minds! What energy and enthusiasm; what spirit! At last they are old enough to understand, to appreciate, to converse, to exchange ideas, to take care of themselves, to take care of *me!* Yet, wondrously they are all still living at home. Now this has to be the best time! Or so I thought. . . .

Until the firstborn got married. At a nuptial Mass, in our parish church, with family and friends all present, my husband holding my hand as our son and his bride exchanged vows, I looked at my family:

Lee, the bridegroom, handsome and proud, alternating smiles for Karen, his bride, and nervous glances at his brothers beside him in the sanctuary. . . .

John, Michael, Jim, and Dan, every bit as handsome as their brother in their rented tuxes, more nervous than the bride and groom. . . .

Mary, Peggy, and Ann, our beautiful daughters, dressed in their wedding finery, a little tearful to lose the brother who teased them and loved them and made their childhood both miserable and wonderful. . . .

Our "little ones," Tim and Patrick, at nine and eight years old, little no longer, proudly carrying the Offertory gifts to the altar as the soloist sang "Ave Maria, gratia plena . . ."

My mother, my sisters and their families, my only brother (godfather to the bridegroom, serving as lector; little did we know that in three short months he would go to heaven). . . .

All my loved ones were there, with the exception of my father.

"Oh, Daddy," I silently prayed, "this is what you meant! This is the time. This is the best!"

And I swear my father whispered to me from his heavenly home:

"That's what you think, sweetheart. The best is yet to be!"

Incredible, isn't it? All this . . . and heaven, too!